growing season

Arlene Bernstein

Praise for *Growing Season*

I was captivated by this story of a woman who finds remarkable wholeness through a deep and mysterious connection to her garden. Nature becomes both Zen teacher and sacred guide leading her to transformation.... This is a wise, lovely book that quietly tends the soul.

Sue Monk Kidd
Author of *When The Heart Waits* and *Secret Life of Bees*

With its mysterious ways of growing and dying and not-growing, the earth is our best teacher, as Arlene Bernstein discovers quite naturally and writes about with beautiful candor. I recommend it in the same spirit that I would suggest making soup from your own garden.

Thomas Moore
Author of *Care of the Soul, Soul Mates* and *The Re-enchantment of Everyday Life*

What a great and nurturing joy to read *Growing Season*. Like the garden she cultivates, Arlene Bernstein offers us a rich and hard-won harvest that is not only soul-nourishing, but fun to consume. I especially liked the natural and pleasing rhythm of her writing, the way it quieted me and comforted me and invited me into a spacious and generous presence. A memorable and deeply gratifying book.

Sherry Ruth Anderson, Ph.D.
Author of *The Feminine Face of God* and *The Cultural Creatives*

It is a healing journey into the heart of nature. I am grateful to Arlene for sharing her compassionate heart with the world.

Frances Vaughan
Author of *The Inward Arc* and
Awakening Intuition

This remarkable book speaks from the heart to everyone who seeks a deeper understanding and connection to life.

Eleanor Coppola
Artist, author of *Notes on the
Making of Apocalypse Now*

In our world that is so largely divorced from an intimate connection with nature, Arlene Bernstein's account of growing things while coming to terms with death is both unusual and very moving. I loved it!

William Bridges
Author, *Transitions*

Growing Season celebrates the healing power of gardening and cooking to nourish both body and soul.

Alice Waters
Author, owner of Chez Panisse
restaurant

Arlene Berhstein's *Growing Season* should be titled *Gift from the Land*. The author makes us aware and treasure every aspect of the earth and all things growing. She opens our eyes and our hearts the way Anne Morrow Lindbergh did in *Gift from the Sea*.

Molly Chappellet, author, *A
Vineyard Garden*

growing season

A Healing Journey
Into the
Heart of Nature

ARLENE BERNSTEIN

Wildcat Canyon Press
An imprint of Council Oak Books
San Francisco/Tulsa

Wildcat Canyon Press, an imprint of Council Oak Books, Tulsa, Oklahoma

LIBRARY OF CONGRESS CATALOGING-IN-PUBLICATION DATA

Bernstein, Arlene, 1940–
Growing season: a healing journey into the heart of nature / Arlene Bernstein.
p. cm.
ISBN 1-885171-10-2
1. Bernstein, Arlene, 1940– . 2. Spiritual biography. 3. Self-actualization
(Psychology)—Religious aspects. 4. Gardens—Religious aspects. 5. Nature—
Religious aspects. 6. Grief—Religious aspects. 7. Children—Death—Religious
aspects. I. Title.
BL73.B47 A3   1995
155. 9'37—dc20   95-12583
                                                                   CIP

09 08 07 06 05 04   5 4 3 2 1

Cover design: Nancy Shapiro Design
Interior design: Gordon Chun Design
Illustrations: Catherine Rose Crowther
Cover tile and vineyard print: Arlene Bernstein

Printed in Canada

DEDICATION

For my teachers: Michael, our children and the land

Contents

Preface

Had you visited Mount Veeder Winery any time from 1973
to 1982, my husband Michael or I would have shared with
you the romantic story of how we transformed a prune
farm high in the hills above the Napa Valley into a thriving
vineyard and the almost Taoistic way in which events led us
to have a winery. That was the outer story. It was easy to tell.

But there is also an inner story of how the land
transformed me, with renewed creativity and spiritual
unfolding, after painful loss and lingering grief. By 1975 I
had taken felt-tipped pen to yellow lined legal pad and in
my isolation had begun asking for the first time questions
like, "How am I to live fully and deeply now that life is not
turning out how I imagined and desired it to be?" And
I learned to listen for answers. This is the story of
Growing Season.

The first part, "Seeds," gives the context in which to put my
journey of reconnecting with land, self and creative source.

The second part, "Fertile Ground," records the dialogue

with my environment that emerged from the turning point, when I surrendered to life just as it was. The land on Mount Veeder became my monastery, and the vegetable garden and vineyard became my spiritual teachers. One day the lesson might come from the ants or the earthworms, another day from the tomato plants sprouting spontaneously on the compost pile. They taught me to trust silence, stillness. They demonstrated the creativity and connectedness present when busy-ness and mental reactivity cease. They showed me the nature of change. They planted the seeds of learning to live life as an active meditation.

It was not until this past year, with our return to land in the country, that the third part, "Ripening and Harvest," could be completed. Ending my story any earlier would have been like beginning to pick the tomatoes as soon as the skin turned red instead of waiting patiently for them to ripen fully within.

So I invite you to join me at the beginning of my growing season and join in the discoveries that unfolded. Your circumstances need not be the same as mine for my learnings to speak to you. We all suffer losses and disappointments. We all have times of conflict in our relationships. We all face change, both wanted and unwanted. We all have a place in our lives, a metaphoric garden, that in the tending can teach us, as nature taught me, about living fully and authentically. But we need to cultivate the stillness at our center so that we may listen.

The lessons are as universal as how the grass grows.

seeds

Plant the tree that bears fruit on your soil.

—Henry David Thoreau

Spring 1994

From where I stand, I hear the crunching of brittle oak leaves under the hooves of the grazing deer who virtually ignore my presence, having established this land as their territory long before I or my predecessors laid claim to it. Neither do the gobbling wild turkeys scratching in the pasture pay any attention to me nor the squirrels darting overhead from branch to branch in the oak woods or the woodpecker making a dwelling in a tree trunk with his familiar rat-a-tat-tat. We have just purchased these four acres, perched in the eastern hills of the Napa Valley, and I am clearing some ground so that I may plant flowers and vegetables once we can keep them protected from the deer. I am knee-high in weeds blooming yellow and purple and white.

I pull some stalks by hand and hoe some others. I stop to lean on the hoe handle and gaze out across my panoramic view, letting the warm sunshine and the visual beauty lull me into reverie. I am in no hurry.

Across the valley I can see Mount Veeder crowning the western hills. Between us, the valley is shrouded in fog.

From this new springtime on my new land from this new perspective I can look back across time to twenty years ago when I lived on a ranch on Mount Veeder Road, at a thousand-foot elevation, beyond the narrow canyon with Pickle Creek winding through, just above the fog line. On a day like today I would feel as though I were on an island in a sea of clouds. I would watch the sun coax the dense grayness toward itself in slender fingers and dissipate it with its warmth.

The land on Mount Veeder Road had the same impact on my heart and soul as the sun has on the fog, coaxing me toward life and love, dissipating the dense grayness of grief.

As we were packing in February for the move from our transitional home in the valley between the two hillsides where we lived for over a decade reshaping our lives and our relationship, Michael came upon our wedding album. He told me in the evening that he had been filled with emotion all day, moved to tears from seeing the innocence, freshness and trusting sense of promise in my bridal portrait, realizing how much I had suffered from the loss of our babies and his inability to join me in support. I had yearned for this kind of sharing and understanding decades ago. Because it had not been forthcoming from him then, when I felt so desperate and deprived, I was forced to take a journey into the unknown territory of my own being. As a result I can thank him now with an open and loving heart for his affirmation and acknowledgment of my coming to healing and transformation in a process that has enriched not only my life but his, and our life together.

I had been raised and educated to be somebody's wife and somebody's mother. I graduated from college and was married a year later to a young lawyer with a promising future. We saw ourselves as quite modern and rational in agreeing verbally to a five-year marriage contract prior to making any long-term commitment that would include children or other major undertakings.

In 1968, a year after we renewed our commitment, I gave birth to a premature son who died at the age of nineteen days without ever coming home from the hospital.

My recollections of the experience of David's short life are few: the wall of the incubator between us; expressing milk with a little hand breast pump and leaving it for the nurses to feed him; the irony of reading his birth notice in the newspaper as we waited outside the intensive care ward while he was dying.

I have a vivid recollection of myself wearing an absurd green-and-white-striped seersucker sack dress with a clown ruffle at the neck and bells fastened to its grosgrain bow. I stood at the fish counter in Petrini's Market on Masonic Avenue in San Francisco and told Luigi, who was waiting on me, "The baby died." I remember the disorientation of coming home from the market, unable to absorb the magnitude of losing David juxtaposed upon having to fix dinner as usual.

"Bind the breasts, the baby's dead," I wrote in a little notebook. Its only other entry described family interactions at my father-in-law's funeral.

Michael and I were assured by the medical team it was a one-in-a-million stroke of bad luck. We took a trip to visit my mother-in-law in Pennsylvania; we picked up my late father-in-law's student violin and took it with us to New York to sell; we shopped, ate in good restaurants and defiantly began trying to conceive another child immediately.

After nine single-minded and tension-filled months, I did
conceive, and the pregnancy proceeded without incident
until I began to have occasional contractions in the fifth
month. In an attempt to control the outcome, the
obstetrician prescribed bed rest to term.

Jason was born Friday, March 13, 1970, a full-term baby.
After four joyous hours, we were visited by Dr. Patton, our
pediatrician, who suggested a heart specialist be brought
in, as he detected a sizable heart murmur. Within five weeks
we knew that Jason's heart was incompatible with life, as
one chamber was not developed. No one could estimate
how long he might live. Dr. Patton advised us to take him
home and enjoy him and let the baby tell us what was best
for him. So we focused our attention on the fragile life
entrusted to our care.

Any energy spent in fear for the future, either his or ours,
was energy lost from savoring the joys of his immediate
presence. When I was able to live in the moment without
projecting into the future or mulling over the past, I had the
very new experience of feeling attuned, noticing just what

action a situation required and responding intuitively and spontaneously. Rather than feeling exhausted as a new mother, I was energized, and the connection with him somehow stimulated my creativity. I even found time to photograph and to print in the darkroom.

Jason didn't act as if he were doomed. For ten months all developed quite normally, with the exception that people would comment on his "olive" complexion, the result of cyanosis, insufficient oxygen circulation in his blood.

In the course of that time, we moved from San Francisco to Mount Veeder. It had been a twenty-acre prune ranch when we impulsively purchased it as a weekend retreat shortly after our marriage, despite our rational agreement to stay unencumbered those first five years. In the eight ensuing years, besides farming the prunes, we had begun planting wine grapes. By fall 1970, we had harvested seven boxes of grapes from the first vineyard, enough to make four cases of Chateau Bernstein wine.

In February 1971, Jason was hospitalized. His heart could not take the burden of his efforts to walk. A risky operation was performed attempting to shunt more oxygen through the maladapted system that had developed to keep him breathing. It was not successful. He lay in the hospital in heart failure, kept alive by drugs, until April 21, 1971. When Jason died, I felt as if the best part of me died with him.

Michael and I retreated to the solace of the land. Michael took a year's leave of absence from his attorney position with the Federal Trade Commission, and the two of us put our energies into vineyard planting on a larger scale. His leave from law became permanent as we discovered we could live modestly by growing much of our own food and by sharing a tour guide job at Robert Mondavi Winery in Oakville, each working two days a week. Otherwise, our days were structured around the endless work of planting and tending thousands of young grapevines.

By 1973 we attracted investors, and in that year Mount Veeder Winery was born. Michael had been successful shifting his attention to work as a way of keeping emotions at bay. I witnessed the way the vineyard and winery thrived. It looked like proof that his way was the right way to overcome grief.

After all, we had been taught to pick up the pieces and move on. Our culture in general, and his family in particular, saw stoicism as strength and the emotional display I was used to in my family as weakness. I tried to do it his way. I went through the motions of being helpmate, but within I seethed and churned. I attempted to deny my feelings of loss and emptiness, but they continually spilled over into tears. I was kept at arm's length by the person I most expected to understand. Michael had his "child" in the wine. I still longed for mine.

I kept Jason alive in images. I had a few rolls of developed film from the hospital experience. Whenever I could steal a bit of time from chores, I retreated to my back-porch darkroom to develop prints. Mothers and their sick children. Gestures of love and support. I exhibited the photographs in spring of 1973 in a San Francisco gallery. The show was my memorial to Jason and to the life spirit I saw and felt in the hospital despite, or maybe because of, close awareness of death. I thought it would be my tangible avenue for emerging from grief. I imagined it would free my heart for another child.

Since I was frightened of another pregnancy, I investigated adoption. Michael left it to me. Without his input, I agonized over which of two possibilities would be the least risk, a private out-of-state adoption of a yet-unborn infant or an agency placement, where supposedly there were fewer unknowns. I thought it would be safer to deal with a local agency. In December 1973, three-month-old Max was placed with us. He had been a low birth-weight baby, but agency medical records indicated his health and development were normal. That did not turn out to be the case. In our first visit to Dr. Patton, he advised immediate consultation with specialists. Max was not tracking the doctor's finger. Maybe it was visual or auditory or neurological developmental delay. In the subsequent days, we relived in nightmarish microcosm the process of discovering a serious disability. The pediatric neurologist advised us to relinquish the baby, as he felt there was the possibility of autism, and it would take five years to see if Max could outgrow the problem.

So one bright sunny winter morning, less than a week after we signed the adoption papers, I was returning Max to the arms of the social worker who placed him with us. Michael wanted to demand a healthy infant from the agency. For me it wasn't possible just to make an exchange. I was emotionally drained. I felt as if I were beating my head against the proverbial wall trying to make my dream come true. The universe was trying to tell me something I couldn't for the life of me understand, and I needed to take time out before I opened myself again. It took almost a year before I gathered courage to risk being vulnerable again. By then Michael had changed his mind. "Three strikes and I'm out," he said. "I can't risk the pain again." Finished. Closed chapter.

Something inside me snapped. Every fiber in my being rebelled. How dare he just bow out from my dream when I was being swallowed up in the structure manifested by his! The cumulative effect of denying my feelings erupted like an overflowing volcano on a rampage. Waves of nausea, burning fires of anger. I hated the demands of the vineyard and the winery. I hated the isolation, feeling trapped on the mountain with an uncommunicative stone of a partner. I hated my dependency. I grieved the loss of hope for children and the loss of the focus, creativity and vitality I associated with my experience of Jason.

My friends indulged my self-pity. They listened. They let me cry.

Trapped in circumstances I was physically incapable of running from, I witnessed my mind running wild with escape fantasies. I would travel alone to Nepal to visit a friend whose letters were filled with descriptions of the beauty and mystery of the Himalayas and the discovery of meditation taught by a man named Goenka. Her life sounded so peaceful, so fulfilled, as expansive as mine felt constricted. I would adopt the Nepali child she wrote about. I would escape from Michael, wander alone in the bazaar and have synchronistic adventures, like the woman she described in one of her letters. I proposed we go visit. "Impossible," Michael responded. "Well, maybe just I could go," I gingerly suggested. "That would be selfish and stupid! And besides, we've always done everything together!" he replied. "If two people always do everything together," I heard myself say from a part of myself I barely knew, "then maybe one of them isn't being honest!"

What was honest? I was torn apart inside with contradictory desires, being pulled in conflicting directions. Craving intimacy, I was sabotaging it at the same time. Michael was willing to risk another pregnancy to keep me from leaving. He must have instinctively known that although I was talking about a three-week trip, I would really be leaving him emotionally in an irrevocable way.

"What do you want," my friends asked, "a baby or to leave him?" "Both!" I answered.

After Jason had died, his baby-sitter, with whom he had a special bond, had told me "Jason will let you know" when it was time to give him a brother or sister. One night at the dinner table, for a fraction of a second, I was sure that Jason was sitting in the chair to my left. I envisioned him grown to the age he would have been had he lived, around four years old, wearing shoes and socks and short pants. His hair was quite blond, his complexion rosy, but his lips were pale and his skin translucent, as I had remembered them in death. I was shocked at first, then sad. I shared the vision with Michael. Tears came to his eyes.

Shortly after, wheeling a cart down a supermarket aisle, I swear for a second I was in Nepal. I had walked away from my life, from everything and everyone I knew and wanted to love. When I came back to ordinary consciousness, I was paralyzed with terror. My hands were frozen to the shopping cart, white from the tension of clinging so tightly that I had constricted blood circulation. My stomach felt like a bowl of jelly.

That night I awoke in a cold sweat from a nightmare: I was running away from home to the Himalayas. I was pregnant. Michael was running after me screaming, "Selfish! Stupid! How can you leave me? We've always done everything together!" My womb had a picture window in it. The farther away from home I went, the more deformed I watched the fetus growing in me become. I was sure I was going crazy.

No solid ground. No control. No roadmap for falling apart. My inner turmoil had become so intolerable that being free from it superseded all other desires.

I was defeated in the battle to create my life as I desired it. My thinking, planning, reacting mind had brought me to the edge of the abyss. It could take me no further.

Then my true journey began.

fertile ground

More in the garden grows than what the gardener sows.

—Spanish Proverb

Winter

The real voyage of discovery consists not in seeking new landscapes, but in having new eyes.

—Marcel Proust

 It is early February 1975. It has been pouring rain for ten straight days. Ever since my thirty-fifth birthday in late January I have been walking around with a huge knot in my gut. Deep inside I am struggling with impulses to run away from my life. I look around the quiet living room, dark and dreary in the downpour, and remember the time when the fire blazed cozily in the fireplace and little Jason crawled on the delicate flowers of the Oriental carpet chasing after old Ronald the cat. We were waiting for Michael to commute home from San Francisco, so happy to be with us, his little family. That was over four years ago.

Now the fireplace is damp and barren. The deck off the living room that held the firewood has collapsed. And there is no time to chop wood with ten thousand grapevines to tend.

"Maybe we are meant to stick to grapevines," Michael had said with tears in his eyes after Jason's heart murmur was confirmed just hours after his birth. I wasn't there when Jason died a year later. But I saw him lifeless. I lifted his little hand. It was limp in mine. I kissed him good-bye on his cool forehead. Michael stood at the foot of the bed, stone still, a million miles away. We came home in silence that day to this beautiful hilltop, and he began devoting himself with unshakable focus to completing the vineyard. And so it has become grapevines instead of children, with the exception of the few days Max was in our life before we relinquished him back to the adoption agency.

We work the land unceasingly. Michael falls at the end of the day from physical exhaustion, outwitting the moment sorrow might find its way to the surface. He is working out his grief with the vines. I have found no place for mine.

I feel so lost. Last night I awakened in a clammy sweat from another nightmare. I had run away to the Himalayas. I was on a precipice overlooking a boulder-strewn river crashing so far below me that the water was only blue and white spots. I knew I had to get across that river. The only way was by a flimsy-looking bridge of woven rope suspended in space. It was a matter of life and death that I cross the river, and though I sensed someone by my side, I knew I had to do it alone. I was terrified. My heart was pounding so hard it woke me up.

I could be that six year old I once was, with the same pounding heart, walking home from school for the first time. Then, I came to a big intersection and waited for the crossing guard to help me, but he just smiled from across the street and didn't come. I didn't know what to do. I was confused and scared, ready to cry. A bus stopped and let people off, leaving the door open awhile after the last person. I paid little attention because I didn't want to get on the bus. Finally, in desperation, I stepped off the curb and into traffic to make my own way. Cars had to stop for me, and the guard finally noticed when I was halfway across and took me the remaining distance to safety. What I hadn't understood was that I was standing under a post with a round sign on it instead of between white lines painted on the street. The language of symbols and signs at the time were crosswalks and bus stops, unknowns to me. The signs that might help me move forward at this juncture are just as obscure.

Michael is working today at our tour guide job down in the valley. He prefers to work more days in the winter when the weather is foul so I will work his days in the spring when he needs to do the cultivating. The assumption is that I can work in my back-porch darkroom productively in the rain. Unfortunately, I have no energy or desire for creative work.

Tears well up in my eyes. I wander to the large picture window opposite the fireplace, the result of our having enclosed the old front porch, and I see the downpour has subsided and the air hangs in a limp drizzle. I look out at the rows and rows of vines, shorn of their splendid fruit, bald of their fiery autumn colors, representing endless hours of work ahead. Though they look dead, they are only dormant, and they need pruning to give form and shape to next fall's harvest.

Where is there to go? What is there to do? Intuitively, I know that anywhere I run I will take my confusion and isolation and pain with me. I give up, surrender to my despair.

I feel the heaviness of my body and soul fixed to the spot, leaden and inert. Then, as if in a trance, I find that I have opened the front door, changed my shoes and begun to navigate myself in a familiar direction, onto the gravel driveway, past the terra-cotta drain tiles planted with thyme and geraniums that flank the picket fence on my right, between the olive and wild plum trees that form an arch out to the approach road, down the slight embankment across the road, past the hose bib nearly obscured by rosemary, into the twenty-by-twenty foot plot of earth set apart from the acres of vines by a crude fence made of discarded grape stakes and chicken wire to keep out the rabbits. My vegetable garden. The only place on our twenty acres that does not overwhelm me with its demands, the only place on the property whose schedule is not managed and controlled by Michael. My little separate space amidst the vast parade of vines.

My galoshes stick in the mucky, waterlogged earth as I begin to wander aimlessly among the soggy, neglected remains of last season's harvest. I scan the landscape, making a mental inventory: One lone onion. A few parsley sprigs. Leeks, carrots and celery root are drowning in the cold, heavy earth. The cabbage stalks have collapsed from the weight of the downpour. The kohlrabi bulbs, looking like green, above-ground turnips crowded together, are going to seed because they were never thinned. The birds have eaten the Swiss chard leaves down to the ribs.

In all humility I ask the bedraggled tangle before me, "What can you possibly offer me in the way of nourishment?" And, much to my surprise, I get an answer, "Hot soup!"

I look again. It's true. I just have to see it differently. The potential is there: a small cabbage head, a rescued kohlrabi, chard ribs. The muck makes the carrots, leeks and onion easy to pull out. I gather some parsley, and on the way back to the house, I pinch a few sprigs of thyme and rosemary from the path.

The recipe is simple: Sauté the onion; add broth and simmer the chopped vegetables; garnish with toasted croutons and Parmesan cheese. The steam from the pot warms the kitchen. The mingling fragrances of herbs and vegetables invite me to inhale them deeply.

I set a place at the kitchen table, and I ladle myself a portion of soup with anticipation. The bowl warms my hands as I cradle it to the table. The warmth of the first spoonful as I swallow melts my chilled spirit. It moves to my belly. The warmth and well-being spreads. Holy communion.

Relief. Peace for a moment. I asked and listened for an answer, and it came. Clearly and directly. From where? It was certainly not the place of confusion and turmoil. What else might be right before my eyes were I to see it differently, without trying to push it away or grab it and hold on tightly?

At the moment the garden answered with nourishment for body and soul, I made a commitment. To visit regularly without express purpose. To be still. To be observant and attentive. To keep notes. I didn't know what kind. I just knew they would be different from the kind of planning charts and things-to-do lists that my garden notebooks had consisted of in the past. It was all right with me not to know.

Foraging

Since the weather cleared two weeks ago, it seems that all I have been doing is pruning grapevines. I have hungered to return to the garden, but today is the first day I have had alone without pressure.

The sun is warm. There is a balmy breeze. The wild mustard, which looks so beautiful in the vineyards in late winter as a carpet of yellow blossoms, is bursting into flower. I wander into the garden to forage.

Forage. *For rage?* To forage: to wander and collect; to hunt for food. Nothing in the dictionary about rage. And *courage?* That word derives from *heart*. God! If I honestly look into my heart, I have to feel how much rage it still holds!

The mustard seed has rooted just as vigorously in the garden as in the surrounding vineyard. There it will be cultivated into the soil as fertilizer, green manure. Here it is a knee-high weed. I grab clumps of stems with my two fists and yank them out, taproots and all. The ground is still damp enough to release the roots but dry enough to put up resistance. I can feel my muscles tense in my arms and shoulders and back. I balance myself by spreading my feet wider apart as I bend down to the ground. Centered, I realize I can meet my anger and use it constructively, tearing through section after section of the garden, ousting the intruder. It feels good to release the tension I've stored in my body so long, and soon I am aware I have relaxed, slowed down and am making discoveries.

Under one clearing I find a crop of mache, a small French wild green, called cornsalad or lamb's lettuce here, its two-inch-long light green oval leaves radiating out in rosettes from a tight budlike center. It is a cool-weather crop that has thrived from last fall, offering sweet field salad greens that are delicious tossed in walnut oil and a touch of sherry wine vinegar. But the sunshine of the past week or so is coaxing its tiny flower buds at the tips of shoots to emerge from the stem hidden at the base of the leaves. "You'd better enjoy us soon before we get bitter," the mache seems to be warning me.

Last fall I dug up the whitloof chicory plants with their hairy bitter green leaves, root and all, and I let the plants lie in a pile for a few weeks until the green tops withered before cutting them off down to an inch above the roots. Then I dug a trench and replanted the roots side by side, and I buried the tops under a mound of sawdust around eight inches high and covered it all with black plastic held down by rocks. With the energy in the roots wanting to grow again and the center of the bud straining to reach light, the pure white bittersweet delicacy of Belgian endive is born. When I peek under the mound, I frighten a field mouse who scurries from her nest in what she thought was a protected place. I see she's already enjoyed the tips of several endive that have reached all the way to the top of the sawdust. "Well, you've had your turn; now it's mine!" I say to her.

Nearby I find lettuce and escarole I remember planting in the late summer. Their leaf edges have been pinking-sheared by some brazen California goldfinch. I imagine if the lettuce could communicate with me directly it would express exasperation about my neglect.

"Well, none of us is in the greatest shape," I muse to myself, "but at least we have all survived."

My stomach lets me know with a rumble that it's nearing lunchtime. I harvest some mache and the endive buds and ragged outer leaves of escarole and lettuce for a salad. But before I take the produce to the kitchen, I leave the harvest basket in the shade of the lime tree and search out a length of bird netting from the barn and fix it protectively over the hearts of the greens left intact. I also see that I can transfer the sawdust no longer needed for endive to make a mulch around the strawberries. Even though I am a long way from planting anew, it feels good to notice something I can do for the garden growing at present.

Weeding

There are few times in life when I know just where I've been and just where I'm going. Weeding in the garden is surely one of them.

In the time since I've last tackled weeds, the ground has dried out more, so the mustard stalks I missed will no longer come out roots and all. I need another way to clear the surface.

Michael has sharpened the vineyard hoes so they'll be ready when we need them to clean the weeds from between the vines. They are a bit large for me, but I take one from the shed and grasp the handle close to the blade. I feel clumsy and awkward, but I find a swinging motion that snaps the stalks off at ground level. I know it is a superficial clearing; the roots are still intact. More rain and they might sprout again. In the meantime, the tops can feed the compost pile, breaking down to become fertilizer for next year's garden.

After the mustard, progress is much slower. I get down on my hands and knees, paying close attention to each plant. My focus narrows, for I must be very gentle and careful as I inch along; tiny parsley sprouts have reseeded themselves and miniature wild strawberry plants are sprinkled among them. Some of the weeds are lovely little flowering creepers, defined as weeds only because they are growing in a place where they aren't wanted. Others have prickly stems. I feel my fingers tingle when I grasp one of them, and the sensation remains long after I have let go. Shallot and elephant garlic bulbs and Jerusalem artichoke tubers that I had overlooked when I harvested last fall divided underground over the winter and are beginning to send new shoots to the surface. I open the ground around them. The earth has a lot of clay in it, and when the dirt dries, my hands feel as though I am wearing tight gloves and my fingertips are a bit numb. The mache is going to seed, so if I clear out around it and leave it undisturbed, it will perpetuate itself next fall. I appreciate plants that grow themselves so easily.

The hours flow by seamlessly. I realize how at ease and focused I had been only when I feel a chill in the breeze toward afternoon and the knot in my gut returns. I stop work and give the knot my attention. Dense. Tight. Right under my heart, at the base of my rib cage. I just sit with it, allowing it to reveal its message. It was triggered by my sense that the clouds gathering in the sky may hold a storm and I will be housebound on a gray and dreary tomorrow. Fear. I fear the clutter in my mind if I do not have the garden to give me focus and direction. The clinging vines of memory. The noxious weeds of anger and resentment. The tangle of repetitious fantasies and unsatisfied yearnings. I wish fear were as easy as weeds to pull out and compost. But then the thought occurs: What's under the fear? What if there is nothing? I'm afraid of that too. Fear of space. Fear of change. Even after a glimpse of well-being.

I look again at the clouds above me. All I had seen were their gray centers. Now I see the translucent edges glowing from the sun behind them. To hold the two together, the glowing edges and the gray core. To let them both be present. The day can do it; maybe I can too. After all, cloudbursts and sunshine together make beautiful rainbows.

Grounding

Just as winter and spring weather are playing hide-and-seek, I too am going back and forth between storms of panic and moments of peace. The storms aren't so violent now or so frequent; I have witnessed enough of them so that I am aware they will pass of their own accord if I do not tense up and try to deny or hide from them. But the yearning to run away is still deeply rooted, kindled at the slightest provocation.

I spotted a book on Nepal in the Napa library, and I had to bring it home and read it. I just finished it this morning. The author asks what it is about the Nepalese that draws us "cerebral tormentors" to the Himalayas just to watch them go about their simple lives farming and herding. His conjecture is that the Nepalese embrace the mystery and magic of life against stringent odds. I stare out the kitchen window, musing on how my life feels to me particularly devoid of both. But the sun is shining and the sky is a clear blue, and my noticing them breaks the reverie and brings me back to the task at hand, getting me outside to start tying the vineyards.

I must make my way through the rows of recently pruned vines, securing the dormant fruiting canes to the trellis wires with plastic ties. At first my fantasies accompany me to the vineyard, but soon I establish a rhythm to my work, focusing on the task, coaxing the taut wood gently toward the wire by bending it between my two hands, starting at the crown of the plant and slowly working my thumbs down its length until I can connect it to the wire and fix it without its snapping off from too much friction. My thoughts quiet and I notice my breathing, soft and steady. I feel the sun warming my back and the support of the earth beneath my feet. I imagine myself joining the life force inside the dormant grapevine. I feel all the new energy for yet-to-emerge growth pulsating to the rhythm of my heartbeat, just pushing, expanding, inside that dead-looking wood, wanting so to burst forth into leaf, then flower, then fruit.

Grapevines grow in place. They send their roots deep into the earth and draw up its nourishment, which sustains them for decades, sometimes as long as a century. Each has to grow from its own connection to the source, alone, and only when its growth is firmly established do the graceful new shoots reach far enough to entwine another's.

They show me what I already sense about myself—that the source of nourishment and mystery and magic is not somewhere far away. It is wherever and whenever my senses awaken to it.

As if to punctuate my awareness with an exclamation point, the very next moment I hear the shrieks of red-tailed hawks, soaring majestically above me in their graceful mating dance, the sun backlighting their fan-shaped tails. I am transfixed with awe at the gift of their presence, and for a moment I soar with them.

Pruning

We're finishing up the pruning, finally admitting that it would be far more pleasant for each of us if we did not try to work together. Until today we had been working side by side, and it has been frustrating for both of us. Pruning grapevines involves decision making and our styles are so different.

When Rafael first introduced us to the principles of cane pruning years ago, he impressed upon us that each year you prune, you are not only selecting the fruiting wood for this season's crop, you are also making the decisions for the following year by the selection and placement of spurs, short pieces of one-year-old wood with only two buds on them. He explained that two or three grape bunches are formed on the green shoots that grow from buds on one-year-old wood, which the previous year had been a green shoot itself, but over the summer had slowly become hard, smooth and light brown. The canes, as those one-year-old shoots of ten to fifteen buds long are called, were tied to

trellis wires and had become fat and grown bark in that
second season when they bore fruit. The green shoots
where the crop had been had now turned to wood, a tangle
tied to a wire that is the first thing you must saw off at
pruning time. What remains after the canes are cut out are
the vigorous shoots that grew from spurs. Because spurs
only make a few bunches of grapes, they put their energy
into green growth, which ideally gives them the girth and
location for the following year's fruiting canes and
replacement spurs. Rafael pointed out the importance of
the direction the buds on the spurs are pointing, so that the
shoots are well positioned for replacement canes and spurs.

I can tell when I am pruning a plant Michael pruned last
year. I feel constricted in not having enough good wood
from which to make good decisions. Michael is decisive. He
assumes he is in charge. He rarely leaves more than one
spur choice from which to make next year's canes. He
assumes everything will grow according to his expectations.

Michael, on the other hand, complains when he meets a
vine I shaped, that the amount of wood on it is excessive. I
always leave an extra spur or two. I like to have options,

"just in case." After all, a shoot may grow in an awkward direction, or get damaged, or be too spindly or too fat even if it is well placed.

The frustrations with our conflicting approaches won't change as we meet the other's mark on the plants, but at least from now on we won't each physically be there to witness the annoyance the other is expressing.

Michael has chosen to work in the oldest vineyards. They remind us of our naiveté and innocence when we started this project over a decade ago. Vineyard #1 is Bessie the Cow's pasture, around the first curve in the approach road winding up the hill to the house. It was the only place Mr. Moyer, Bessie's owner and the old farmer we purchased the ranch from, hadn't planted plums or prunes. Mr. Blackwell, a prune picker who stayed on after the harvest, living in the Civil War vintage cabin where the winery now stands, brought home two bundles of discarded cuttings from a vineyard-planting job down in the valley. He had lost the tags, so we had no idea what grape variety they were. With Bessie gone, the logical place to put them in the ground was the pasture, three buds buried in the earth, two buds above the ground. Imagine our amazement when all but two of them rooted and began to grow vigorously!

Michael was stimulated to begin reading viticulture texts. The first thing he learned is that you never plant the European wine grape varieties on their own roots because they are susceptible to the root louse, phylloxera. He immediately contacted the University of California at Davis. They were experimenting with making grafts of the preferred wine grape varieties on pest-resistant rootstock, and they agreed to sell Michael all the cabernet sauvignon grafts after they collected their data. For four successive years, they supplied us with somewhere between fifty and three hundred vines annually. Pulling out the fruit trees one by one to make room for vineyard was the task of every weekend from summer through fall. Michael would attach one end of a chain to a tree, the other to his Caterpillar 28 tractor, a machine as old as he, and they'd pull. When the tree was uprooted, he'd take his chainsaw, cut it up for firewood, and haul it back to the house. Then he'd run over the land with a disk and a roller to smooth it, and we would take pegs, string and a level and make contoured rows.

After the rains, he'd dig holes, I'd plant the vines, dig a trench around each one with a mattock and then water it to settle it into its new home. The vineyard size was determined by the number of vines the university gave us.

Michael has assigned me to prune what we call the "problem" vineyard. Its problem is that the vines are different ages. We tried newly developed greenhouse bench grafts, where nurseries inserted a bud of cabernet sauvignon into a cutting of phylloxera-resistant rootstock and in the protection of a controlled environment coaxed the roots and the green shoot at the same time. The plants came in little collars and were set out in the spring rather than the old-style dormant bare-root plants put out in late winter before new growth began.

The first time we planted, half the tender plants cooked in a heat spell shortly afterwards. The nurseries hadn't understood in those days that they couldn't take such tender specimens force-grown in protective environments directly into the real world with all its uncontrollable randomness and extremes without hardening them off— that is, exposing them little by little to expanded temperature ranges. So we replanted and replanted through that growing season and the next until there were no empty spaces. All that time, the survivors of the first plantings grew without support wires until the youngest vines needed them. Consequently, the shapes of the older plants are unorthodox. There is no way to use pruning rules on them.

This gives me great freedom, with no judgments attached of right or wrong, too much wood or too little. I give myself permission just to stand before each plant, quiet and empty of thought, until I get a visceral sensation, almost an invitation to join in a dance. Then, slowly at first, I'll cut out the fruiting canes from last year, but not always back to their beginning, as the rules dictate, because it's just as likely I'll find the best new canes are the shoots that grew at the base of the old. And then I wait for a quickening as the vine and I communicate, as one shoot or another catches my eye and I accept the invitation or not, clearing out little by little those which give me a visceral "no." I'm able to prune with imagination and intuition, visualizing each plant as a sculptor might view a piece of wood or a block of marble, just asking the form to emerge.

When we finish pruning, we will have a break in the work schedule while Michael waits for the ground to be ready for cultivating. It's a chance for a long overdue vacation, but every place we have talked about going has caused the same difference of opinion that gets us stuck when we try to adapt to each other's pruning styles. We have chosen Hawaii by default; we were both neutral about it. At least that allows us both to go with no particular expectations.

Creating Space

 The lettuce seeds that I scattered in hastily prepared ground as a parting gesture before we left two weeks ago have all sprouted. They have made their first true leaves and are crowding each other as they continue to grow. They cannot all expand and mature in such suffocating closeness. Since I haven't yet turned the soil, I have no place to transplant them. Thinning is the only answer.

My fingers feel clumsy and invasive as I work my way through the delicate leaves, trying not to disturb the plants I want to grow. I poke until I find the base of the leaves at soil line, and I try to pull the entire seedling out. Sometimes the miniature head snaps off, sometimes a slender white root comes out of the soil with it. I try not to bruise the tender leaves with too much pressure, but it is very hard not to crush some or tear some, releasing milky white liquid.

Just as I am opening space for the lettuce to grow, I realize that Hawaii gave Michael and me a chance to explore space in our relationship. We were together, but separate. Michael was absorbed in reading Michener's *Hawaii* and I was reading Anne Morrow Lindbergh's *Gift from the Sea.*

I walked alone on the rocky shores of Hana on Maui, not far from the Lindberghs' beloved seaside retreat, hunting my own seashells, exploring tidepools teeming with billowy flowers suctioned to the rocks and black porcupine-quilled creatures embedded with coral and shells. My steps were tentative in flimsy rubber thongs on the uneven terrain. I noticed a bright blue snail cross my path.

I brought him back to our room to get to know him better. I watched him move so very slowly, venturing timidly across the kitchen countertop, retreating into his shell at the first sign of contact with an outside element. I wondered at the amount of time he spent all curled up inside his shell, alone, peeking out only after he was sure all danger had passed. I admired him for carrying his home with him. Self-containment. But I also could sense the extra weight as a burden. Outside I had watched him make his way across the rocks, creating his own pathway. I admired that. But even then, he had cautiously surveyed the terrain before he explored it, and the range of surfaces he was comfortable upon was limited.

Michael and I, too, were cautious of the ground we explored together, retreating at the first signs of obstacle or disagreement. I realized how much my self-image has been tied to being right, to being agreed with. I had been conditioned to believe that I would find my identity through marriage and a loving husband who would care for me, define me. No wonder disagreement got mixed up in my belief system with rejection, which is tantamount to not existing. No wonder I retreated into my shell. Our complete sharing of the past years since Jason's death has been my clinging to Michael's direction like the billowy sea anemone clinging to the rocks.

Lindbergh quoted the poet Rilke:

"A complete sharing between two people is an impossibility, and whenever it seems, nevertheless, to exist, it is a narrowing, a mutual agreement which robs either one member or both of his fullest freedom and development. But once the realization is accepted that, even between the closest of human beings, infinite distances continue to exist, a wonderful living side by side can grow up, if they succeed in loving the distance between them which makes it possible for each to see the other whole and against a wide sky!"[1]

Rilke wished for a change in relationships between men and women, which he hoped would no longer follow the traditional patterns of submission and domination, possession and competition. He described a state in which there would be space and freedom for growth, in which each partner would be the means of releasing the other, a love in which "two solitudes protect and touch and greet each other."[2]

The separation between us in Hawaii felt like a taste of that new potential, not the old self-protectiveness. There was space, but it was peaceful space, unfraught with tension and defenses. We respected our differences.

One day we hiked to a pristine pool below a waterfall, through a quivering giant bamboo forest. I was tagging well behind Michael. The tall timbers swayed and creaked in the light breeze. The sunlight splashed through the shadows as we penetrated the darkness. The earth was not solid but a tangle of bamboo roots floating like a matted carpet in a swamp. I felt ripples pass under my feet, though I was standing perfectly still. Then a shudder passed through me, leaving me tingling, weightless, as though I might fly. I dared not breathe; I didn't want to miss a whisper. The sparking sunlight ignited my skin. Boundaries disappeared. My toes became dancing bamboo roots, and I throbbed with the same life energy as a new bamboo shoot about to reach toward the sun.

As it passed and I realized that I had been transported to another way of being, if just for a moment, all I could do was laugh. Laughter as the sunshine was laughing through the tall bamboo. I chuckled to myself, "So this is what it feels like to be really alive, to be connected! This is what I dreamed I might find by running off to Nepal, and here it is, right here, right now, and the source was Michael's footsteps ahead of me!"

When we reached the pool and splashed playfully, stripped to the skin, it felt like a baptism, a celebration of rebirth.

❧ Not only have I made space for the remaining lettuce to expand and grow, I have enough gleanings to make the ultimate delicacy, a fresh spring salad. I take the thinnings into the kitchen and fill one of the sinks with water, and I immerse the little seedlings briefly to separate any clinging earth. Washing salad greens from the supermarket may sometimes be a chore, but washing newly grown seedlings from the garden is an act of love.

❧ I signed the guest book at the Lyman Museum in Hilo, our last stop in Hawaii, and wrote March 13. It was the first time that day I realized it was Jason's birthday. It was the first year in the last five he hadn't filled my thoughts completely on the day.

Lindbergh used the argonaut shell, named after the mythic ship the ancient Jason set sail in to search for the golden fleece, to symbolize the stage of developing a mature relationship. The creature who inhabits the shell (the argonauta, or paper nautilus) is not actually fastened to it at all. The shell is a cradle for the young, held by the mother who floats with it to the surface, where the eggs hatch and the young swim away. Then the mother argonaut leaves the shell and starts another life.

I know that I will not be able to bring maturity to relationship until I feel whole within myself. I felt most whole as mother, but now I must find my creative fulfillment in some other way. I sense it is time for me to set out on that new journey to find out who I am apart from being Michael's wife and Jason's mother. The shell that cradled my Jason is empty. I was taught that being loved would make me whole. I feel loved, but now I dare to ask myself the question, "Do I love?"

"How does one learn to love?" a scholar once asked a holy man. "By loving," came the answer.

Now is the time to begin. It is only a refound self who can refind relationship. I know I must journey alone, even if the distance is short and the pace is that of a tiny bright blue snail.

Journeying Alone

 The wind is gathering force in the foliage of the gently swaying redwoods and is sending puffy white cumulus clouds across the blue ground of sky. Today it feels as if spring may finally be on the horizon, but there have been so many false starts this year. We've even been pelted with a passing hailstorm and a steady sequence of rainshowers that manage to continually postpone the possibility of cultivating the vineyard or turning the garden soil.

Yesterday we bottled our first commercial wine, Mount Veeder 1973 Cabernet Sauvignon, Bernstein Vineyards. I thought I would be excited, but instead it just felt natural. Of course all will go well. Of course the wine shows great promise. Of course we will find enough friends to help out if we are short-handed.

I was assigned the filling machine, eight spigots revolving in a circle. With only 375 cases total, I dared not be slower than the machine or wine would spill out, and any loss was a large percentage of the whole. At first I was awkward, but soon I got the rhythm of reaching for an empty bottle with one hand and sliding it under the spigot at just the moment I was removing a bottle at the proper ullage, or fill level, with the other. I rather enjoyed the repetition of the task. The bottles clinked and rattled as the cases of empty ones were dumped to my left and the full ones continued on at my right to the steady "c'plunk" of the corking machine. The winery was damp and chilly. The bottles were cold. My hands and feet were freezing. But the spirit of cooperation and the camaraderie made up for it.

❦ With the vineyard pruned and the ground too wet for cultivating and the wine in the bottle, Michael is going to paint the fence and I am feeling free to go off for five days. I will head first to San Francisco for a baby shower and an art exhibit opening and then drive down to the Monterey area, three hours south of the city, for time alone. We got a notice in the mail that J. Krishnamurti, the mystic philosopher, is speaking at the Masonic Auditorium in San

Francisco the same day as the shower, so at the last minute I decide to attend that, too.

Annie B., my mother-in-law, sent us Krishnamurti's book *Freedom from the Known* after David, our firstborn, died.

> When you lose someone you love, you shed tears. Are your tears for yourself or for the one who is dead? When you cry for yourself, is it love? Sorrow and love cannot go together. So when you ask what love is, you may be too frightened to see the answer.[3]

Truth is a pathless land, he says, so you cannot depend on anybody—no guide, no authority—to show you the way. There is only you, your relationship with others and with the world. If you just look, he says, you see a unitary process, which I visualize as a figure eight, inner movement expressing itself as the outer world and the outer world reacting again on the inner. And he challenges us with the question, "Can you then, seeing this whole picture, not verbally, but actually, can you easily, spontaneously, transform yourself?"

He calls the process "choiceless awareness," observing without judgment just "what is," how the space between "what is" and our desires for it to be different is the place where we suffer.

When I arrive I am amazed at the crowd pouring into the auditorium. The only seating left is in the balcony. The man sitting next to me says he has been coming to these talks for thirty years, so although the words have a straightforward simplicity and make sense, the actions must be difficult to practice.

At precisely eleven A.M. Krishnamurti walks onto the stage, which is bare except for a straight-backed chair. He is a man of slight build in his late seventies or early eighties with a regal and commanding presence and an impeccably tailored suit. He seats himself in the chair and begins to speak in a voice equally regal and commanding. There is no palpable warmth in his presentation that invites attraction to him personally. He purports not to be a teacher. He considers the talk a mutual exploration. He refers to himself as the speaker, not "I."

What he calls meditation is not concentration. It is being aware of every thought, of every feeling, never saying it is right or wrong, just watching it and moving with it. In that watching, you begin to understand the whole movement of thought and feeling. And out of this awareness comes silence. And into this silence, it is possible that love will enter. Love cannot be cultivated by thought. It comes on its own when thought ceases. All one can do is see what it is not, put one's house in order and open the window on the chance that the gentle breeze of love will waft through. Meditation, choiceless awareness, is like opening the window.

After the talk, Krishnamurti invites questions, but he seems impatient with the questioners, as if they have missed his point entirely. Since he maintains that freedom comes when one stops seeking, when one ceases to look for answers outside oneself, I suppose speaking to large audiences of seekers is bound to create a bind. I have no questions. My life has given me the curriculum for Krishnamurti 101 and more, and I just have to do my homework!

❧ Joanne's shower in the afternoon gives me an opportunity to meet several of her friends from her professional life as a well respected exhibiting photographer and art professor. It is a window into a world in which a part of me has always dreamed of participating. The art exhibit opening I accompany her to in the evening brings me face to face with the appearance and reality of that world. I have never been surrounded by so many people who call themselves artists. Joanne introduces me as a wonderful photographer, and I get responses like, "Oh, yes, I've heard of you," when they obviously haven't but better not admit it in case they should have.

I remember as an art student thinking that the whole point of creating art was to gain recognition. One evening in the printmaking studio at UCLA I chanced to have a conversation with Kiesho Okayama, a fellow student who had been in a Zen monastery in Japan. He said he painted in order not to need to paint. I couldn't fathom what he was talking about. At that point I had given myself a decade in order to be validated by the world, and if I didn't make my deadline, I was going to give up trying. How ironic that when I did exhibit, it was to memorialize Jason and the intense love I witnessed in the hospital. The work had nothing to do with putting out a product or gaining personal recognition; it was a heartfelt process.

Krishnamurti says that art divorced from life has no great

significance. "To be creative is not merely to produce poems, or statues or children; it is to be in that state in which truth can come into being."[4] I knew I was in the presence of truth when I witnessed the images in the hospital that compelled me to record them.

✢⁄ Joanne joined me on the drive to Monterey and we spent the evening together, but now that I have left her at a conference, I have a day to "just be" before checking in to a weekend retreat.

I watch my timidity driving toward a puddle in the road to Julia Pfeiffer Beach, a small cove across the highway from the lodge in Big Sur where Michael and I stopped on our honeymoon. I park at a safe distance before it and walk to the beach, while others meet it boldly and splash through.

It is a sparkling day. The sea is crashing in powerful waves against the shoreline sands and the huge boulders that frame the beach. The wind whips the froth from water flying in the air. Blowing sand sparkles with a wine-colored sheen. The waves cross and come together, then retreat in separate directions. Clouds merge with the sea's horizon, the two forming a continuum of misty blue.

Though we strangers on the beach are all enveloped by the same wind, we each relate to it from our separate worlds. I am huddled in my sheepskin jacket, battling face to face. A free-spirited little boy chooses to dance with its rhythm, letting himself be blown to and fro. A young woman who has found a sheltered spot in a crevice of rock suns herself in a red halter top, oblivious to the wind's force. And a laughing family uses its energy to sail a Frisbee in a rowdy game of catch.

I observe how uneasy I am about having unstructured time. I have brought all my props along to fill it: sketchbook, journal, cameras. I try sketching, then writing, then looking through the viewfinder. It's all an effort. I choke on the self-conscious trying.

When I finally witness the impatience and greed of needing to seize something of the environment and the anxiety that I won't "make something out of my time here," I give up pushing myself. I find a perch on a rock. I notice the rhythm of my breath, feel the solidity and coldness of the rocks supporting my weight from under and behind me. I open to the power, energy and vastness of the turbulent ocean, the merging of clouds and sky on the horizon. I turn to the green hills behind me, which appear pulsating and throbbing under a blanket of haze. I realize I am hungry. I take out my picnic, really paying attention to the tastes and textures of what I am eating, and then I settle back, relaxed, to drift into a nap.

Only when I awake refreshed do images come alive to me, beckoning to be recorded in the camera's eye: rich warm-toned striations in the boulders, pockmarks in the sandstone that from a close perspective could be craters of a volcano, sand swirling around miniature dunes that could be mountains emerging from a vast desert. I work effortlessly, joyously. The playful family spontaneously includes me in its game. Father, in his hand-crocheted tam-o'-shanter throws the Frisbee my way, and I, in turn, pass it on to his son, whom I've heard him call Jason.

Alive. Connected. Again and again I get the same lesson. It is not a factor of place but of my attitude, whether in fear needing to control or in trust being open and receptive to life's unfolding. Letting go is a prerequisite for letting in.

❧ I need to find a place to stay tonight, so I go to a cafe to use the phone. It's very quiet now, and the hostess joins me for a cup of coffee. She cheerfully offers to take me home with her, if she had a home. I'm intrigued to hear more. "Oh, one morning I woke up and looked at my boring dentist husband and my conventional Junior League existence, and I just walked out on it all. At the moment, I'm crashing on a friend's floor, just floating, and it's magic." She sounds like the woman in Nepal whose freedom was a magnet to me.

When she asks about me, I tell her that I needed a bit of vacation from marriage so I came here alone to get some space, that I've signed up for a meditation weekend and I'm just getting to know myself a bit, that I've had urges to just take off like she did, but I didn't have the courage. "Oh, it doesn't take courage to split," she responds, "anybody can do that. It's really you who has the courage for seeing your needs within your relationship and taking care of yourself without leaving anyone else in the lurch."

My search for a place to stay is discouraging. The lodge and the inn are both full, and the only place with room is a damp, dreary cabin smelling of mildew in a tacky motel.

Having had myself mirrored by Lynn as courageous, I decide I don't have to stay there to prove anything to myself, so I call old family friends who are happy to have me on their couch. I'll have enough time with myself at the retreat.

❧ Now it really is just me. A small room with a bed, a chair, a lamp and four bare walls. Meals scheduled. Three scheduled group meditations and the rest of the time sitting with my body, my breath, my thoughts and my feelings.

The novelty of having time alone wears off quickly as I witness the agitation and restlessness of my mind searching for something to focus on other than my breathing. Time expands. What I hope is an hour turns out to be only four minutes. I stretch, I wiggle, I pick at my cuticles, an old nervous habit. I still have hours before me. There is constant chatter from a judging voice inside; it mocks the

irony of my self-pity for being isolated on my beautiful
mountaintop and then leaving to come here! There is also a
voice that sounds like Michael critiquing the food and the
accommodations, but Michael is nowhere around, so I have
to own it as mine. And when I finally do settle down to pay
attention to what is happening inside me, the predominant
sensation is an intense pounding in my forehead behind my
eyes, a dull, throbbing, relentless ache. It feels as if my brows
are furrowed, straining to see something elusive. I watch all
my reactivity. I could get an aspirin. I could lie down. Make
it go away. I hate it. I watch how all the reacting against it is
creating more tension. So here is the experiment, the
challenge that Krishnamurti put forth. *Can you just look,
without judgment, at "what is?"* When I stop tensing up
around the discomfort I notice something extraordinary.
The pain is not solid. It is alive and varied in depth and
intensity. Sometimes it is so dense it feels like an invading
foreign army. Then it will change to a concentrated point of
stabbing with a diffuse web around it. Another moment it
will just be a dull gray fog. Another like a steel vise gripping
my head, making my eyes feel too big for their sockets.
Then when my attention shifts to images playing out on the

television screen of my mind, I don't even notice it. The same scene replays over and over, and I feel as vivid an emotional response from the trigger of memory as if I were in the middle of the scene. Every now and then, for what feels like a few seconds, the screen goes blank and I am aware of breath coming in, going out, the sensation of heart beating, cells pulsating, life living itself on a moment-to-moment level. Day and night, mostly the headache, the memories, the emotions, the physical sensations coming and going, tedium, anxiety, pain. I look in the mirror. I see the truth. I am thirty-five years old and grieving deep inside. I am witnessing the pain of struggle to have it be otherwise. The tears that come are a relief, a cleansing.

I awake on the morning I am to leave noticing that the headache has left, and I feel lighter and happier than I can recall feeling in years.

There is very little change in the weather or the garden when I return home. But for the first time I find myself irritated with the overgrown tangle in the front yard. The time in retreat was like an inner spring housecleaning, and I feel compelled to create more space and order in my environment. I tackle the weeds, a task I have never until now seemed to have time for, and I am rewarded by discovering violets and iris that have patiently struggled to survive under the clutter. Now sunlight will be able to reach them and they will flourish.

Michael senses my new buoyancy. Over a lunch of salad from more lettuce thinnings, he asks with a long face, "Why are you always so happy away from home and so unhappy here? Maybe you are a masochist. Maybe you don't love me anymore. Maybe you want a separation." I answer from a newfound place inside me, "Our first marriage is dead, but I'd just as soon you be my second husband!"

Spring

Sitting quietly, doing nothing,
Spring comes, and the grass grows by itself.

—Zen saying

 In the vineyard the grape buds have broken their protective covers, and the first cottony swellings of new life are emerging. Soon the new shoots will unfold and burst forth.

I am standing quietly in the carpet of cover crop yet to be cultivated. I see the clover begin to pulsate at my feet. Pop! comes the head of an earthworm. Then he sways and wriggles the rest of himself up until he is scooting atop the grasses. I imagine the scale changed. He becomes a giant snake promenading along treetops. A moment later from a spiked thistle, out pops the head of a rust-colored slug. I feel certain that if I could be truly still I would hear the mushrooms swelling deep beneath my feet.

Waking Up

 Last year I started some asparagus seeds in an old fruit crate in the potting shed next to the garden. They sprouted and survived the summer without much care from me. When they went dormant I moved them to an abandoned vineyard row between two clumps of redwood trees. As I settled the crowns in the rich humus, I couldn't really believe those stringy pathetic rootlets had any life in them.

In winter I poked around a bit amidst the weeds that overtook the spot and I did find a few; in fact, I decapitated a few in the search. Before we left for Hawaii, I stopped to check progress and I discovered one, two, three. But I had planted fifty-seven!

Today the sun is shining and I pass by again. Miniature asparagus shoots, no broader than a blade of grass, are waving in the breeze. I stoop to greet them and open up their space, pulling out the miner's lettuce, which comes out easily, and making a half-hearted attempt at some of the tougher weeds, using my hands where I really need a hoe.

As I inch along, I realize almost all the asparagus shoots have grown. "How happy I am to see you all!" my heart sings. They bring me face to face with how difficult it is for me to trust.

"Where is your faith, your patience?" they ask me. "Just because all you saw was a seed or a stringy root crown doesn't mean that's all there is. It was only a stage in our development. You were so worried that your efforts would go to waste. But you weren't the one controlling our growth. It is the sun and the air and the earth and the water that are unfolding us. Some plants make showy blooms in a very short season; others grow very slowly. Our first efforts only hint at what maturity will bring.

"Be patient with us slow starters. Be patient with yourself, too. Trust the seeds sleeping deep inside. They shivered through stark, cold weather, drenched in winter's tears. But because of that very moisture, when the warm sun reaches them they will be pulled magnetically until they burst through to air and light. Our seeds become asparagus, but yours—you will have to learn from listening deep within what will germinate and grow for you."

Sprouting

 Today I feel in harmony with the universe. The basil, tomato and eggplant seeds I planted in tofu containers on the window-sill have all sprouted simultaneously with the tomatoes and zinnias on the compost pile.

Cultivating

Usually, as human beings, we are not interested in the nothingness of the ground. Our tendency is to be interested in something which is growing in the garden, not in the bare soil itself. But if you want to have a good harvest, the most important thing is to make rich soil and to cultivate it well.

—Shunryu Suzuki Roshi

I have been paying particular attention to the earthworms. Making fertile rich soil is just their nature. Their lot is undramatic. They ingest the earth, digest it, change and enrich it as they go about nourishing themselves. They point me into my garden ground.

There is very little space for new beginnings with the stubble of the old still covering the ground. Room to plant anew appears only as ground is cleared and opened up. My garden soil is not a virgin plot. Besides the old weeds, there are the fragile and spotty beginnings of volunteer annuals and the dependable regeneration of perennials. Some need to be incorporated into the ground, others need to be worked around. The soil needs to become receptive.

My work is to turn it over. In some places the earth is still waterlogged and resistant. In other places it is light and friable. My work is the same for both. Push the spade down, bring up ground from the deep, pull it up with the spade, turn it over, bringing the depths to the surface. All of it, no matter the texture, is teeming with life. Not just earthworms, but pill bugs, slugs, beetles and Jerusalem crickets all are going about their business. I am engaged in what seems, from my point of view, like a profoundly symbolic act. From theirs, however, I am a nuisance upsetting their domestic tranquillity.

My garden ground, in turn, has pointed me to the depths of inner ground surfacing through dreams. One, in particular, has been particularly compelling:

I am planting shrubs around the winery. The ground near the building is tough and impenetrable, so I start digging in the more crumbly, friable soil around the creeping myrtle. I reach into the dense ground cover, and I'm bitten by a snake. It's on my wrist, so if I cut it open to suck out the venom, I risk slitting an artery and bleeding profusely. Michael is running the tractor on another part of the ranch, so he can't hear me if I shout for help. If I run to where he can see me, I will circulate the venom through my system and it will be more deadly. Both cutting out the venom and leaving it to circulate feel tremendously dangerous.

The surface dilemma of the dream is familiar—the fear of having to make my own decision without help and not trusting it to be safe.

But the snake image continues to pursue me in my daily life. In all our years on the property, I have rarely encountered a snake. But now I find a shed snakeskin in the garden, and I come upon the most awesome meeting in the front yard: two rattlesnakes entwined, undulating and writhing vertically, supporting their entire weight on their slender tails. They are so absorbed in this mysterious ritual that they do not notice me, and I stand transfixed in the power of their dance and the energy of their joining. It is as if I am witnessing a live caduceus, embodying both healing and poison.

The symbolic snake invites me to go with him into his familiar territory, the depths. I don't know what this means, but I trust that he will guide me.

✣ It's a week now since the snake has been hovering in my consciousness. Today is the anniversary of Jason's death. A rumbling thunderclap, then gathering clouds and now hail and rain have sent me scurrying into the house with the cilantro I was harvesting. The pungent aroma acts like a bridge back to memories, to the *albondigas* soup at El Cholo during Michael's and my courtship in Los Angeles and spontaneous lunches of raw fish salad at Sam Wo in San Francisco when we were first married. Back and back I go, into childhood. The downpour turns to showers, with thunder and lightning, and I find that I have committed my life story to paper, twenty-two pages of patterns, repeating and repeating, in which Jason's death and how I am living its aftermath are just another example.

Every step away from home, ever since I can remember, has been accompanied by guilt and fear. Independence, discovering myself, trusting my inclinations and intuitions have somehow become paired with abandoning someone whom I love, who loves me. When I married, I exchanged an old dependency for a new one. Fear is the family heirloom, passed down through generations to my immigrant grandfather to my mother to me.

Another powerful dream image I have been holding becomes clear, of a police chief's wife who is buried alive in an Egyptian tomb. I am the buried woman, buried under layers of fear and guilt and deferring to external authority above my own inner knowing.

Can I shed those constraints as the snake sheds an outgrown skin?

Planting

 Winter is the mourning of beautiful Isis for the body of her beloved husband, Osiris. The earth, in response to her bereavement, grows barren. She continues her search for his coffin and at last finds it aided by Ra, the Sun God, who brings him back to life. With his resurrection, life returns to earth. The Nile swells, and growth returns to plants. Buds swell and hope returns. And the planting festival is the most sacred of ceremonies.

—Egyptian myth

I am like the calligrapher who must first meditatively grind his ink before making the deft sure stroke with brush or pen on the blank white sheet. My medium is earth. My preparation is to gently crumble the clods between my palms, lightening the texture so it will welcomingly receive the seeds. Some places need more moisture, others more time. Still others ask for a top dressing of compost to lighten the tilth. I do not have a plan. I panic with anxiety for a moment. Where do I start? "Stay calm and attentive," the earth assures me. "You needn't impose a plan; it will emerge." I relax. Stand still. Breathe deeply. I let in the sensations of the sunshine bathing my skin, the sounds of busy insects buzzing, the perfume of the waxy white lime blossoms and the solidity of the earth beneath my feet. And soon, like a magnet, I feel pulled first to one spot, then another. Tomatoes near the lime tree. Of course! Squash next to the fence. Garlic near the lettuce. Beans next to the strawberries. It's as if each plant knows its best home and just has to lead me to it. I am merely the vehicle.

Letting Go of Expectations

"What is your inspiration?" Andre Kostelanetz asked Matisse, then aged eighty, when he marveled at his still productive output of paintings. Matisse answered, "I grow artichokes."

—*The Art of Contentment*

ᔰ I planted spinach seeds three different times. The first ones never sprouted. The second and third times the slugs ate the new sprouts. I mourned the spinach. And then, today, after having given up on them, I see zinnias and cosmos flowers have volunteered in the spinach row.

ᔰ I spent the morning pulling weeds for no reason but to feel the earth in my hands. It was light and crumbly and shook loose easily from the hairlike purslane roots. The rest of the day I worked on my chosen spot for a carrot row, beating it into submission. I lugged sand up the hill from the winery in my garden cart, feeling short of breath from using all my weight and energy to counter the uphill grade to the garden. I strained it and turned it into the heavy clay clods. They broke down to smaller clods, but clods they remained. I used the mattock and the hoe, and still they resisted. I imagined myself in the position of a carrot root, struggling in such an unyielding environment, ending up twisted and gnarled and stubby from the constant obstacles. Finally I gave up in disgust. I stared into space, exhausted, frustrated with my failure. Then I turned to leave, and there in front of me instead of behind me as it had been all afternoon, was the perfect place, friable and weeded, made ready effortlessly this morning!

❧ I was struggling along in the darkroom printing a black-and-white close-up portrait of a head of cabbage. The critical voice inside started undermining my confidence and my concentration. "No good; waste of time!" it harped. I became uneasy and finally stopped. I washed the dishes and folded the laundry, and shifting gears helped me relax. When I returned, instead of picking up where I left off, I let my eyes wander over some bits and pieces of collage material I had begun years before. Lo and behold, they began combining themselves anew, and I finished three collages, having fun doing them!

Trusting

The weather is warm and summery.
Yesterday a hot, dry north wind ripped
maliciously through the vineyard, tearing
off tender vine shoots that had opened
their tiny white flower petals and released musky perfume.
The heady aroma is almost intoxicating.

I walk the rows inspecting the damage. I have to trust the
secondary buds on the fruiting canes to recover and replace
the valuable crop potential that has been destroyed. And I
have to remove the suckers, nonfruiting shoots that just sap
the energy of the plant. I move from vine to vine with
trowel and mattock and pruning shears, digging patiently
and deeply at the base of each vine to get to the source of
those nonproductive shoots. If I become impatient, just
yanking them at surface level, they'll surely return. Even
rubbing the easy shoots from the trunk or graft union with
a flick will not remove them. Two dormant buds will come
to life for the one I remove. It's necessary to cut carefully at
the base to remove them, too.

In the crown of the plants I can sometimes see new growth that will be crowded out by other shoots, making it impossible for them to get enough sunshine to mature their fruit. They aren't well positioned for next year's fruiting wood, either. If I take the time now, I can rub them off easily with my fingers, opening up the heart of the plant to the shape of a candelabra.

It is becoming clear to me that sorrow and fear and guilt have been like suckers, draining energy from my heart and spirit. Those deeply rooted feelings don't "rub off easily." Patiently meeting them over and over at the level they emerge is the only way to find their source. But I wonder, if I were to notice less deeply rooted reactions at the time they sprout, might they respond to one quick flick of awareness and be gone?

Expanding

 A hummingbird hovers; a garden snake shades itself in the shadow of the broad sorrel leaves. The sun is climbing higher in the sky on its way to summer solstice, sending its blessings down on my garden as well as the vineyard. Early crops that lived through the winter are bearing their harvest and challenging me to reassess limiting attitudes.

My strawberry plants are either being fruitful or they are multiplying, but they are not, as the Scripture says, doing both. Those who are not putting all their energies into ripening their fruits and giving us a feast every morning are sending out runners that root new plants and increase the population. They show me there is more than one way to be creative, productive. If I value only the current harvest, I will miss appreciating the abundance being created for the future.

The Swiss chard I planted last fall is at the height of its prolific output now. It is one of the most reliable garden crops I grow. The only problem is that Michael does not like Swiss chard, and Michael is not generous about eating what he does not like, even if I put effort into preparing it. I was taught to eat everything on my plate.

I like chard. I always feel so virtuous when I eat it, giving my body all the vitamins and minerals I know it contains. But the sense of guilt that I was brought up with—think of all the starving children—now extends beyond the dinner table and into using everything that grows in the garden. And even one chard plant produces more than I can consume. I'm never successful in disguising the chard. Michael has antennae that identify it even in minuscule quantities.

I realize I'm imagining hiding chard purée in the ricotta cheese layer of lasagne that I'm preparing ahead to serve at the grape harvest dinner in the fall. With all the company present Michael wouldn't dare complain. I realize how devious and manipulative I am willing to become when I feel powerless to have him accommodate me. Just because

he doesn't enjoy chard doesn't mean it wouldn't be
enjoyable to others. But there is no way to share the
abundance with others and accommodate him as well. For
him it would be simple. If he were cooking and I told him I
didn't like brussels sprouts, for example, he'd probably not
cook them even if he liked them. There is no way I can hold
on to my old conditioning and accommodate him at the
same time. I plant chard, I face this bind.

Being Constructive

 The beans are beginning to climb. They need support. Same for the tomatoes. I find some old wire fencing. I string a stretch between two posts for the beans, and I shape the rest into cages for the tomatoes. It's not my favorite activity, but I'm aware of a need and consequently feel obliged to respond.

I watch myself as I work. I am impatient at first and clumsy with the wire cutter. I feel all the resentment of having said "yes" to something, when I would have preferred to say "no." My fingers burn as I push them against the unyielding wire to loop it back onto itself. I can feel a blister forming on the side of my thumb from friction with the cutting tool.

As I reach the halfway point after an hour or so, I become bored and have to exercise discipline to keep plodding ahead. I persevere, and my resistance to the task drops away as I find the easiest way to roll out the chicken wire and the best place to cut so that the edges twist around each other easily to hold the cage together. Then I get more adept at the twisting motion and find a kind of rhythm, so that the last cage is as easy and satisfying to construct as the first one was unrewarding.

❧ There is a gopher whose mounds dot the eggplant row and a mole who systematically tunnels under the basil. I can't seem to interest Leo, the stray cat whom I adopted, to take any interest in either. Instead of cooperating with me to keep the plants protected, he goes after a lizard who keeps the insect population down. He struts proudly with the lizard's tail and two hind legs dangling from his jaws. Then he torments a garden snake who is shedding his skin. The snake is so stunned I have to help him back to safety in his hole. Maybe once the snake regains his composure he'll take an interest in eating the gopher or the mole. Or maybe everyone will just do as he or she pleases in the scheme of things. I humbly submit to the possibility that my desire to influence the course of events has no impact whatsoever!

Summer

Be patient toward all that is unsolved in your heart . . .

—Rainer Maria Rilke, *Letters to a Young Poet*

 The miniature grape bunches have set. They will grow, then slowly begin *veraison,* the process in which the skin turns from green to transparent to deep red as pig- ment develops that will give the wine its color.

Michael's job is to get up before dawn, before any breeze begins to blow, and to dust the vineyard with agricultural sulfur to inhibit mildew. The acrid smell of sulfur lingers in the air, burning my nostrils in the heat of the afternoon, which, fortunately, thanks to our elevation in the Mayacamas Mountains, is cooler than it would be down in the valley.

I do not have any assigned tasks until the harvest, just the continual maintenance of the vines. I walk through the vineyard from time to time to take care of recurrent suckers or to tie any canes that may have fallen loose or to hoe the occasional recurrent weed that has sprouted since cultivation.

I have time to just be. Time to join the garden, the soil, the plants and the diversity of creatures that make up its universe. Time to discover my place among them.

Reassessing Obstacles

 Purslane is by far the most bountiful crop growing in the garden. It takes hold in every open space in the planted rows and between them. It's a friendly weed, no prickers or seeds to stick in my socks, and it's pretty, with fleshy bright green leaves creeping along the ground, but it's a weed nonetheless. Last week I tried pulling it out by its roots where the ground was moist and hoeing it where the ground was dry. I threw it in a big pile outside the garden fence. For three days the garden had a well tended look that made me feel a bit smug about being master of my universe.

This morning as I meander through the beans and poke through the melon leaves to see if any fruit has set, a rosy sheen on the path catches my eye. On closer inspection, I realize that thirty-five trillion little purslane beginnings have regenerated. For every conquest I had shaken as I pulled it out, a million new replacements have been born. It's time to rethink my attitude.

Now I'm researching recipes for purslane salad and cream
of purslane soup. I read in *Organic Gardening* magazine
how purslane's vitamin A and C contents are superior to
many domesticated green leafy vegetables. But harvesting is
a problem. When it's small and succulent, it is virtually
impossible to pick and clean, and once it's large enough to
pull out easily, it is covered with yellow flowers. Another
book says that purslane helps domesticated plants reach
their roots down to food that would otherwise be unavail-
able to them. As a weed it is a nuisance. But how about as a
companion plant? A yellow flowering walkway? A succulent
mulch? A rich repast for the compost heap?

꙳꙳There are cucumber beetles on the beans and slugs in
the mulch. And gophers and moles are burrowing underground. The moles don't mean any harm. They just topple
young seedlings that they happen into while searching for
bugs to eat. If I see their damage early, I can always tamp
the earth down again before the plant roots dry out. But
gophers are out to get the plants, stripping the underground portion of plant stems and eating the roots. I've

heard they will pull entire plants down into their holes. Actually, none has done any particular harm in my garden yet, so I hold no ill will. That's why I shuddered at the suffering I caused when I speared a gopher accidentally while poking the earth with a spading fork.

At the same time, though, I was rather fascinated to see this creature who had heretofore eluded me. Even though he was wounded, he was alive and struggling with all his strength to return underground. The cats and dog were attracted to the commotion, but none of them would pounce and finish him off. I finally put him out of his misery with another spearing, then I buried him.

From now on I prefer to coexist. The gophers can enjoy stripping the roots of an occasional basil or eggplant, and I will consider their mounds a contribution of perfectly textured potting soil.

Exploring

 I like to sit in the shade under the lime tree
in the corner of the garden even though I
have to share the spot with ants who have
always lived and worked here. So when I
read some garden authority who said that mint repels ants,
I immediately planted mint all around the tree. Now the
mint is wandering far afield, making a green path that I
must constantly thwart to keep it from taking over. The
worst is that, far from repelling ants, it seems to have
invited them to take up residence. So here I sit watching the
mint pulsate with busy ants, white specks of larvae in their
mouths, running up and down each stem and then disap-
pearing into the same holes into which they've always
disappeared.

I've read that most ants are dull and stupid, following trails
left by others, doing their work farming aphids and carrying grubs, crawling along, sometimes bumping antennae to
say hello or pick a fight. The workers are all females. The
males just mate with princesses, then die. Princesses

become queens: living longest, staying put, making eggs, getting fat.

But there are also a small number of bright, energetic females, "excitement-centered ants," intelligent leaders of their communities. They explore and make new trails, then return home to point everyone else in new directions. That's the kind of ant I'd like to be.

But what if the scent of perfumed fruit led me out of the garden and to a kitchen countertop, and with one swoop of an almighty sponge the trail and I were erased? I recognize that thought as a contribution of my old companion fear, reminding me that adventure involves risks. The real question is, how willing am I to go exploring new directions, fear and all?

Observing

It is a quiet time. Cool-weather crops have bolted to seed, and the summer vegetables are slowly unfolding and coming to formation and ripening. I wander slowly among the wonder of life and nature just being itself, observing randomly.

❧ The bees are busy gathering nectar from the blossoms, leaving the miracle of fertilization behind, totally unaware that they are the catalyst for transformation. Soon little green spindles will emerge as beans, and little green bumps will grow to melons and tomatoes and cucumbers and eggplant.

The bees are just gathering food to make honey. Being who they are, doing what they do. The same is true for the yeasts that transform grape juice to wine. All they care about is eating the sugar in the grapes so they can make more little yeasts. Unself-conscious creativity.

❧The potatoes are flowering white replicas of the yellow tomato blossoms, and the eggplant are making lavender ones. It's clear at this moment that they are all family.

❧A gentle rain is falling unexpectedly. It reaches down and caresses the plants, spreading its blessings evenly. All the blossoms are sparkling, and the leaves are stretching wide and shining a brighter green. The rain is watering the garden in such a different way than the garden sprinkler, which does battle with the plants, leaving them bent and drooping, beaten down by its force, with beads, pearls, crystals of water dripping from every leaf.

Opening

I have a personal question for the zucchini: "Do you think someday I might be able to give forth prolific blossoms of rich gold, like you, and have my fruits mature?"

I hear an answer in my heart: "Your flowers will not be like mine; they will be your own, the shape and color and fruit unique, unseen while still in a protective coat of bud. The inside must swell and become too full to be contained. Then the shell is no longer needed. The center can burst open and feel the warmth of the sun directly and expand in the freedom of space.

"The process is quite impersonal. I am a blossom just once on a plant that bears my brothers and sisters, in a row of brother and sister plants; we are joined in the garden with others far different yet involved in the same unfolding, connected across time to the plants who bore the seeds last season that we grew from, and our seeds which will grow next year's garden. We are at the same time uniquely ourselves and interconnected manifestations of life itself, as are you." The answer feels as if it has come from the source of us both.

❧The bushes are raining green beans! A shy bachelor friend was over helping me pick them yesterday, and he blushed, "You remember being single, don't you, how it's either feast or famine?" "Do you think that changes when you're married?" I answered.

Now this morning I see scores of beans that we either overlooked yesterday or that have literally grown overnight. I poke slowly through the green on green. They aren't easy to spot. In fact, I can't really look for them at all. They are camouflaged like wild mushrooms in a woodland carpet. They teach a lesson in not seeking too hard. They seem to say, "Look openly, gently, and we'll appear. Look from more than one perspective, too—first from one side of the plant, then from the other. From above and below. And never be sure you have us all! There'll always be another you can't believe you missed."

❧Michael was angry with me when he left for the vineyard this morning. He snapped at me. He slammed the door loudly as he left, and when he came back for a tool he forgot, he just glared silently.

I can't seem to let go of my defensiveness and resentment. I bring them into the garden and take them with me under the lime tree to sit quietly. I feel the tenseness of my shoulder muscles, the tightness in my jaw, clenched and accusatory, as in my mind I alternate between invective and noticing my breath. Into my head pops the word *tunafish*. It breaks the hold my reactions had on me and brings me back to the present. "Now what does that have to do with anything?" I ask myself.

I set about harvesting beans (*tunafish?*) and puttering amidst the rest of the vegetables. I lift the potato mulch and there are tiny new potatoes *(tunafish?)*. Green beans. New potatoes. Tunafish. Salade Niçoise!!

Instead of making an ordinary lunch, I create a beautiful platter. Michael returns at noon braced for my usual vindictiveness and instead finds that I have created a peace offering. I feel the power of having consciously chosen to affect the atmosphere by letting go of ill will. Michael responds with festive affirmation.

❧The first green peppers of the season are ripe. I already anticipate heartburn and flatulence as I chop the peppers and peel the garlic, but my mouth waters in anticipation of the oily, garlicky, subtle spicy flavor of the marinade.

The recipe for Moroccan chermoula: For every two green peppers, combine roughly five cloves of garlic, whole but peeled, approximately one teaspoon of paprika, two pinches of ground coriander seeds, one-fourth cup vinegar, one-half cup olive oil and salt to taste. Slowly simmer the chopped peppers in the marinade. In about twenty minutes, the pepper chunks are cooked, the marinade is concentrated, and if you cool it in a sterile jar, it keeps for several weeks in the refrigerator. Serve as an appetizer, in a bowl, so you can mop up the marinade with crusty French bread.

A cast-iron digestive system is a prerequisite for warding off repercussions, but I for one have never denied myself the sensual pleasure of chermoula on the basis of future payment for my excesses.

❧Peanuts don't want to grow for me. My soil isn't right, even though I deposited wheelbarrow loads of fireplace ashes in the rows and worked them in diligently. Not enough moisture? Too many burrowing critters? Did something eat the seeds? The few seeds I put in a flat in the potting shed did sprout and the plants grew. A few days ago they even had orange pea blossoms. But today I notice they're all shriveled up.

In my non-peanut patch right now is a radiant array of volunteer zinnias. I also planted some zinnias in the front yard. I have visions of the yard slowly coming alive with color.

I've always admired the front yard of the woman who lives around the first bend on my way down the hill to town. She has cultivated a dazzling rose garden and dahlia bed. Now there's a "For Sale" sign on the house. After years of investing all that love and attention in her flowers, she will be leaving them. I wonder how she can do it.

I envy the order and perfection she achieves by limiting her scope. But another part of me finds the repetition of the same garden every year boring. That's why I tried peanuts—for the newness, the unknown.

Most of my vegetables now are knowns. Take green beans, for example. They do well here. They like my garden. I give a certain amount of energy to harvesting them and making them good to eat. I toss the tiny ones in butter and fresh herbs. I make marinated bean salad of the fat ones. And the fattest I purée with butter and lots of garlic. That dish is so good that a prominent Napa Valley wine grower known for falling asleep at the table stayed awake through an entire dinner party.

While musing on cultivating known and unknown vegetables, I'm taken by the realization that something new is growing in me: sitting on the edge of silence, with an open and accepting heart.

Romaine Lettuce

Water trickles down white ribs
Out crawls a tiny spider.

Dreaming

 I am in the garden serenading the vegetables. As the bow moves gracefully over my cello strings, the rich vibrations cascade through the air and the plants pulsate with life. The melons blush yellow and pink through their green shells; the zucchini swell; the green beans stretch their slender fingers; the tomatoes peek from behind their leafy curtains. Over it all, dancing rhythmically, are the bright warm colors of cosmos and marigolds, and yellow-and-black-striped butterflies and bumble bees are darting in and out.

The jackhammer tapping of a woodpecker on the oak tree outside the bedroom window awakens me. The cello disappears. I bound out of bed to shoo away the noisy bird. I am drawn outside to the first rays of sun rising over the hills and the last glimpse of the full moon sinking behind the redwoods.

In the garden the birds are raucous amidst the tangled August abundance. Goldfinches are nibbling at the new melon leaves. Robins, linnets and tanagers are pecking in the mulch around the base of tomato and squash plants. The whole profusion is bathed in the unifying backlight of early sunshine, almost convincing my doubting eyes that plants have glowing auras.

The garden is literally my dream come true, and I feel its glowing energy ignite my heart.

Forgiving

 I am admiring the tomatoes this morning, noticing the just-visible green fruit with its first blush of pink. Suddenly a signal goes from my eye to my brain to my hand holding the pruning shears, and green guts pour out of a tomato hornworm. His casing shrivels and writhes like the dying red balloon in the movie classic, and he hisses the tomato hornworm death rattle.

"What have I done?" I ask myself in horror. Then I look carefully for the first time. His chartreuse body is covered with fine hairs and striations that could have inspired a Navajo rug design, parallel lines of black and white zigging at an angle down one side of his back and zagging up the other. At the end of each pattern is an eye-shaped exclamation point. He has a red tail. Or is that his horn? I realize I don't even know which end is his head.

I still hear chirping, squeaking. There's an army present! I see black pellets in many of the tomato leaves, cylinders formed like miniature corn on the cob. I listen for the enemy to locate its whereabouts. Cat and mouse. I wait. I spot one. Advance! A poke. A prod. I try to make him move. He is mute. I get impatient. Off with his head!

The involuntary squirming in the two hornworm corpses does not stop. If I watch, it will make it harder to continue a search-and-destroy mission. If I get to know the enemy too well, if I see the life in him, I may begin to respect his right to exist. I may lay down my weapon.

"Hey, what's the purpose of this garden, anyway? You growing it to feed the bugs?" a belligerent inner voice demands. "Do the job! Defend your territory!" I am intimidated.

Three. Four. Five. Six. Snip, squish, oblivion. I tuck them under the mulch so I don't have to look. But they're in the next plant, too. A stronghold is already established.

"See," the voice badgers, "time's running out. Get in there and finish them off!"

I hesitate a moment, step back. With distance, I see one I missed; he's clinging to a half-eaten leaf. I haven't disturbed him, so he doesn't know about the massacre. His back is arched; the little protrusions are holding his food. He's completely still. Does he sense my presence? Nothing happens. I wait. He stays perfectly still. I lose patience. I attack.

Silence. The dead are strewn about the ground. Vestiges of their living presence, the black turds, are still in the leaves. And some of the runny innards that spilled before the worms fell have begun to turn from green to black upon exposure to air and sun.

Across the path is another tomato patch. It's clean. What a relief! I've seen enough of the violence in me made manifest.

An hour later, I cannot resist returning to see the hornworm corpses. Shriveled like accordions, baking in the sun, innards spilled, they still writhe and emit squeaks. I watch the gasps from the front two pincers that feed the mouth. These pincers are black, while the others are the same green as the body. The excitement-centered ants have discovered the hornworm flesh and have already directed their busy comrades to this new source of food. The ants hustle into line. The hornworms squeal.

I take a clear-eyed look at myself: capable one moment of openhearted love, coldblooded murder the next. I am a microcosm of the macrocosm. I have compassion for the lot of us.

I had the pruning shears in my hand because I intended to pick a flower bouquet of yellow, Michael's favorite color, and red, mine, for the dining room table, to symbolize our differing natures creating beauty side by side. I do make a bouquet, but now with every color in the garden, solemnly embracing the entire spectrum existing within the human heart.

Autumn

Everything is gestation and then bringing forth.

—Rainer Maria Rilke, *Letters to a Young Poet*

 What else might I be doing besides harvesting tomatoes, running water over their skins, cutting their tops and slicing them into a giant pot on the stove to heat and stew so I can grind them in the food mill for purée? The abundance in my life at this moment is tomatoes, and my creative act is to make tomato sauce.

I may dream of expressing my soul with poetic imagery, but the fact is that what I have to share these days reaches others through their stomachs.

Nine eggplants are waiting to be arranged in a casserole once the tomato sauce is ready. I have a virtual eggplant assembly line, slicing, blanching, draining, sautéing, then tucking the slices between layers of tomato sauce and cheese. I'll put the eggplant Parmesan in the freezer until the grape harvest, when it will nourish the harvest crew.

Maybe my inspiration in the garden and the kitchen will fuel the fire of someone else's creative imagination.

❧ Today it is obvious how the recipe for ratatouille was born: All the ingredients are ripening simultaneously side by side in the garden. Ratatouille came from a garden walk with a basket on one's arm: an eggplant here, two zucchini there, some peppers, basil, tomatoes. Onions and garlic from the kitchen cooler, herbs from the border of the garden walk.

I know people who pride themselves on following recipes to the letter, running all over town to get the proper exotic ingredients. But it seems to me that the most satisfying results come from creatively combining what's at hand.

Harvesting

 Friends have come for the grape harvest from as far away as Los Angeles, bringing their friends. That is how Bob is in my kitchen, as adorable as I remember him from fifteen years ago when I had fallen hopelessly in love as we danced at Merle and Howard's wedding. He is in his jockey shorts, leaning up against the sink, enraptured as Michael explains how he punches down the cap of seeds and skins into the fermenting cabernet must. I confess to him how heartbroken I was when I learned of his engagement shortly after that wedding.

"Oh, it's much better this way, believe me," he teases. "Otherwise there wouldn't be these wonderful grapes to harvest and this wonderful wine."

Over the weekend I scrutinize his wife. By Saturday afternoon she has taken charge of the harvest, giving everyone assignments and reprimanding anyone who drops grape bunches in the dirt or fails to pick a vine clean. Michael likes her a lot. They have quite similar personalities, actually. I find her assertiveness and authority intimidating. Bob operates more the way I do, being generally charming and not quite so productive, allowing himself to get diverted from the task at hand any time there is a kid to play with or a baby to hold.

The whole weekend is a celebration. The weather is mild and clear. The grapes are at that perfect state of ripeness where the bunches snap off easily or yield to the slightest touch of the crescent-shaped picking knife. The pickers' spirits are high. The children are in ecstasy working alongside their parents and being allowed to stay up late for dinner and sip wine made from the variety of grapes they have picked. Thimmaiah has invented a pickup cart from the frame of Jason's baby carriage, which he found in the woodshed; he is wheeling boxes of picked grapes to the ends of the rows. Seeing the baby carriage with grapes instead of a baby brings tears. It takes me back to our first and only harvest with Jason, propped up in the carriage, watching us proudly process our seven boxes of grapes by hand. But there is too much in the present to allow me to stay in the past. Jason is here only in my heart.

Naomi and Larry stay in the house after our lunch of salade Niçoise and ratatouille, doing all the dishes and even washing and waxing the floor. Alice arrives late in the day, decked in a sunbonnet, the picnic basket over her arm, laden with baguette sandwiches filled with Provençal ham, sardines and tomatoes drizzled with olive oil. Claire takes some apples home down the hill after we finish picking and returns with apple tarts as the grapes are being dumped into the crusher.

This is Michael's first harvest with full responsibility for the winemaking as well as the vineyard, as our partner of the last two years bowed out, and by the end of dinner he is exhausted. Our houseguests and I are all energized and stimulated by the day's activity, and we keep talking and enjoying each other's company far into the evening. We document Michael's participation on the tape recorder, rhythmic snoring from the couch as backdrop for our festivities.

✤The grape harvest is completed. The still October afternoon is bathed in golden light, alive with the magnified buzzing of a yellowjacket, who drinks from a dewdrop caught between the leek leaves, and of the honeybees hovering around the garden hose. Amidst the abundance of monarch butterflies I see a new kind, its wings a watercolor wash of brown-black with a line of white calligraphic dots and a cadmium yellow exclamation point at the tip. The sure-handed brush stroke of a master.

The tomato harvest is at its earnest peak. I held on to all the volunteer plants as security, letting them grow wherever they sprouted, and I appreciated their early-ripening fruit. Now I see there are enough others so that I need not be greedy. I pull up one large cherry tomato plant and gather the fruit to process for the freezer. Under it are three toads, bewildered and squinting in the unfamiliar glare of sunlight. "Change, my friends, that's just the way it is!" I attempt communication, giving each a gentle pat on his tough, leathery back. "You thought you were secure, but it was only an illusion. I know the neighborhood appeared quite stable for months, but you were just lucky." They are only annoyed, shrinking back as if to accentuate their dis-

pleasure at the inconvenience I've caused them. No point
now in apologizing or even trying to be helpful. I've
uprooted these three, and that's my relationship to them at
the moment, like it or not. They are homeless, and I have a
superabundance of tomatoes.

Why not a tomato celebration? I've been cooking tomato
dishes all day long. I'm in the mood to share them rather
than just put them away in the freezer for the future. Sure
enough, with a few phone calls, I get together a spontaneous
party. We'll have tomato soup garnished with curried sour
cream and chives for a first course, and eggplant and tomato
casserole for a main course, and tomato and basil salad after,
all accompanied by our own wine. For dessert we'll have ripe
Perlette grapes and Red Delicious apples off the land. For a
table centerpiece, tomato sprigs and zinnias in bouquet, and
for party favors, a huge ripe tomato at each place.

Michael teases me about how silly it all is. I ignore him.
Everyone has a wonderful time. Charles says the meal is delicious, and Lili is annoyed at him for enjoying the same
things at my house that he refuses to eat when she serves
them at home.

Sharing

 Tree-ripened apples fallen to the ground are the sweetest. I have to cut out the rot and sunburn and bugs, but what is left makes delicious slices to be baked under a crumb crust. They look ugly lying at the base of the tree; they'd probably never be appreciated by someone who didn't know. They'd surely be shunned in a fruit bowl. But their flavor is ethereal; one bite is worth five fancy tarts made from store-bought apples or even from the early varieties on the old tree that was here when we bought the property.

These apples are from the trees we planted soon after we moved here, trees that grew and blossomed but never bore fruit. We tended them but became discouraged at their barrenness. We gave up. Then one day when we had no more hope, they burst forth with an ambrosial abundance.

Share the abundance. The first crisp bite is delicious, but if you gorge on the crop, you'll get a bellyache. Nothing is wasted, even if the apples rot at the base of the tree. They will decompose into fertilizer. But I want to share. Give away or transform by baking and freezing. Make food for others. It's hard work harvesting and preserving. It takes commitment.

I have the urge to see my inner experiences take on a new life in tangible form, to be spread beyond the reaches of my personal presence, to find their way from beneath the tree, so to speak. But the harvest is still in its raw form. I need to salvage the nourishing parts, find a recipe, and arrange the ingredients.

My experience with the apples may give me the direction I need. I have pored over elaborate recipes that use apples, but most were just vehicles for performance. Instead I've chosen the simplest way to use lots of fruit. Apple crisp: essence of apple. Just a hint of cinnamon and cloves tucked under a sugar, butter and ground walnut crust.

Letting Go, Again

 There's a fall chill in the air. The north wind is flapping and clanging the loose tin on the barn roof, announcing that the season is changing. The oak trees let go of their leaves, and the wind blows them across the house roof with a crinkling sound. The autumn reds and yellows of the grapevine leaves are at their height. The neighbor's vineyard is looking bare, so it won't be long now for ours. One killing frost will turn the leaves crisp and brown, and they, too, will fall.

I wander through the garden witnessing the wane in activity. An eggplant or two is forming, and a few tomatoes might still ripen, though the majority are squishy and a bit rotten and the plants have mildew from the early rains. Still struggling to push from the ends of the zucchini vine are small yellow flowers and miniature fruits, even though the younger leaves are sickly yellow green and the old ones are crisp. I know I should uproot them all and tuck the earth to rest with a blanket of composted grape seed and skin pomace. But I can't quite bring myself to let go entirely. It's not so hard to pull out plants that are completely expired, like brittle cosmos and zinnia and dried bean plants or the new melon vines and bean and tomato sprouts that were tricked by Indian summer into thinking it was growing season. No matter how late the frost, they could never mature. Under them I find mole holes that were camouflaged by summer's tangle and huge cracks in the earth where the hot sun had drawn away the moisture and shrunk the earth back, exposing the depths.

Under the melon are volunteer mache plants that I never would have found if I hadn't cleared some space. My mother always says, "Old doors are closing and new ones opening, but if we dwell on the old ones, we don't see the new ones all around." If I could bring myself to uproot all of last season's crops, I'd be able to plant a winter garden. I do spade a few areas, and my imagination begins to picture winter lettuce and escarole.

The bare earth itself no longer creates anxiety. It looks inviting. I have learned to trust its emptiness. But I watch how I still cling to the last shreds of life in so much of last season's crops. I know this applies to my inner life, too, with its memories and plans and desires and imaginings. I'm just learning to trust letting go within.

Opening, Again

 The air smells like chocolate and medicine
from the new walnuts I am husking. I am
thinking about how little one can tell
about the nutmeat inside from seeing the
green husk and how protected the heart of the nut is by the
tough outer shell.

Earlier I tried shaking the green nuts from the tree and
forcing the husks open by throwing them against the
shed wall to break them, and my fingers got sore and
stained brown from trying to disengage the nutshells.
Now that they've been through a cycle of rain and then sun,
the expansion and contraction has naturally dried the
husks and the shell comes free easily. Nature has it all timed
and worked out. I see how out of place my earlier impatience was.

The same for my heart's protective cover. I need to trust that it has its own cycle for opening again. Patience and compassion for myself in the interim are the inner components equivalent to rain and sun for the walnuts.

❧I am chilled to the bone despite the warmth of the gaily blazing fire in the fireplace. Rain showers are being whipped across the gray sky by a raw wind.

I ventured out for only a short time this morning, to pick tree-ripened persimmons. And now, on the kitchen table, I am enjoying a visual feast.

Several weeks ago the persimmon tree leaves turned yellow and orange, and then they fell, leaving beautiful orange hearts with daintily pointed tips hanging under brittle brown caps from the ends of bare branches. I already picked some hard persimmons and closed them in a paper bag with an apple to help them ripen. They have less pucker and more sweetness than their commercial counterparts, but they bear no resemblance to what is possible when fruit comes to perfection on the tree. It is only after the persimmons have been exposed to a killing frost that they develop the sweet taste and sensuous texture of tropical sunshine.

I am relating the paradox to inner experience and entertaining the possibility that if the same principles apply throughout nature, then the storms and frost of suffering may be the catalyst for appreciating life's sweetness and delicacies.

Loving

The wintry air has an icy chill as the storm clouds ride across the sky on the wind. If it rains, it may turn to hail or snow.

I'm raking leaves. My movements are awkward and stiff from the layers of clothing—undershirt, turtleneck, sweatshirt, then parka—that I'm bundled in to keep warm. Even though I wear two pairs of socks under my boots, my feet feel frozen. The oak trees are bare, and the damp leaves on the ground collect easily into mounds. I move them to mulch around the base of the incense cedar trees that surround the house.

Out of one pile pops a toad, looking for all his winter camouflage like a live leaf. I apologize to him. He eyes me suspiciously, makes a giant leap, then stops dead still. I see him so totally blended into his environment that he is indistinguishable from it. "Well, what's the secret," I ask him, "to living so naturally in harmony?" We stare at each other in silence. I hear a voice in my heart answer. "It's not what you do but how you go about it that is the secret. What you grow with love will grow you, too!"

᳕The oak tree next to the house has burst forth with fungi, great fans unfolding from slender stems, making a stairway at the base of the trunk. I call Joyce, my knowledgeable friend, to come identify them. She finds them in her book: oyster mushrooms, rated "edible, choice" for eating. She is overjoyed. I give her a big sack to take with her.

She tells me how happy she is that Mother Nature gives us unsought bounty at our door because we give such love to our grapes and vegetables.

While I am sautéing the mushrooms for our dinner, I wonder, "Can we give such love to ourselves and each other?"

Pruning, Again

 No matter the particular conditions of the individual year, certain rules have been elevated to ritual. Cultivating always takes place after April 18. Mr. Moyer, our predecessor, picked that date because after the Great Earthquake of 1906 there was a huge rainstorm. Thanksgiving is the official day we start pruning, rain or shine. Michael established that rule. It is a fitting way to honor the holiday, and, fortunately, the weather has always been clear and sunny, though it is a thinner, paler sunshine that heralds the coming of the shortest day of the year.

We are working together. He accepts my style now that the problem vineyard entrusted to me had the best tonnage in the harvest. We share what is on our minds. He queries me on business decisions. I express my feelings: I don't have a clear sense of how to channel my energy creatively if I am to remain childless. I express the recurrent pull to venture into the wide world, not as a means of escape from our life together, which was the original impetus, but now as some unfulfilled longing in me to be addressed and honored. He says he understands. We work quietly, side by side, shaping the vines. Occasionally we consult each other for help with a particular plant, but more and more we trust ourselves and each other with the decisions we make.

I remember back to a warm sunny day in early November when I hiked up Mrs. Pieromarchi's hill across the road and was able to see the broad panorama of our domain. As I gazed out over the land from that perspective, the vines cascading in contoured rows down the steep hillsides, their leaves at the time all the warm colors in the spectrum from yellow to red-purple, I saw the ability of the land to metaphorically reflect my life as it truly is.

The first thing I saw was the wide asphalt apron off the county road leading to the old green metal farm gate. Right inside is the small winery. Our outer face to the world.

At the top of the hill around the bend, flanked by redwoods and incense cedar, tucked under an umbrella of majestic oak trees, is our house, its basic structure a solid log cabin that has weathered many storms. It is unpretentious and in need of repairs but basically it is still sound, cozy and inviting. It has the same properties as our marriage, the shelter from which the partnership has overseen the transformation of the land around it from prune orchard to vineyard.

I could see the two open areas still in the vineyard, one on either side of the hill. One had vines on it that were destroyed by a landslide. Its instability has kept us from replanting again for fear of loss. It represents our experience with children. The other was never planted. It contained a gaping landslide that we terraced back into place. It still needs mending, but nothing serious. It is lying fallow, like the part of me that longs to journey both far outside the vineyard fence and deeper toward my own center. From the broader view, each of these areas nestles comfortably in the company of the healthy, productive vineyard surrounding it.

The garden, the heart of the land for me, as the vines are for Michael, wasn't visible from Mrs. Pieromarchi's hill. Though I couldn't see it, I could acknowledge its teachings: to be still and attentive, to witness without judgment, to be open and accepting of the natural cycles of growth and change, to let go of preconceptions and expectations, to appreciate abundance in whatever form it comes. I am aware of how the garden has given me insight, but I also realize that insight is not in and of itself living the awareness. There are still so many layers of inner ground to penetrate. The garden gave me back my center, and now from a sense of that center I can come out to meet the whole.

As I work silently beside Michael, trusting myself as I shape the vines, I notice their patterns of growth. Each vine started with a top pruned to two buds, one of which grew, supported by a stake, to be the eventual trunk. Which shoot it would be and how long it took to achieve the necessary height was an individual matter, depending on its vigor. In the next stage, the direction of the shoots growing from the young trunk determined how useful each might be for an eventual productive arm. Slowly the plants took shape. Some grew very traditionally, following expectations; others ran into problems, doing the best they could within their limitations.

There is a period of active growth once a vine's basic shape is established. Buds push their green shoots in the spring.

They reach for support while they are tender and new and vulnerable. If the rate of growth is too rapid while the shoot is fresh and new, then it might topple from the plant under the strain of its own weight, especially if the slight breezes turn into a north wind. The plant has auxiliary buds in reserve as self-protection, so the wound heals and the plant can recover. Moderate growth is more successful in the end. A gentle, steady growth gives a shoot a chance to strengthen its bond and toughen even as it reaches out. It can then support its own weight, even if it does not find the support of the trellis. Paradoxically, the more it toughens, the more flexible it becomes, so that it can survive a twist or a split or an attack of north wind. To flower, the plant must not be growing too rapidly, for energy must be balanced in order for the flowers to set fruit.

Now, at this time of the year, once the fruit has been harvested, the nutrients have been drawn deeply into the root system to be stored for future growth, and the foliage has fallen, exposing the structure. It is the time for choice, for shaping the future growth by cutting out spent parts of the past.

The lessons of pruning are to see the plant as a whole and to let its inherent form suggest the possibilities for its new shape. We must choose a direction opening out from the center, remove the timid, spindly growth that has never matured and the overly assertive shoots too busy gaining length and girth to flower fruitfully. Seeing the whole. Opening out from the center. Balance and space. Moderation. These are the pruning principles for vines. They are principles I can now include as well, as teachers for my own growth, just as I am able to let Michael back into my heart.

ripening and harvest

Start at the place where your own feet stand.

—Zen saying

Winter 1995

New Year's Day 1995: A light rain is falling. The clouds are low and dense, sealing off our sanctuary, so that the world outside appears to end beyond the fringe of green trees outside my window. We have lived on our new property nine months now, becoming acquainted with what we inherited and making it our own, beginning to fill in the boundaries with our dreams and plans.

Yesterday Michael finished laying out the grid where he will plant his pinot noir vineyard in February, and he began driving in the support stakes. It will be a miniature of the past, four hundred vines, spaced close together like the vineyards in Burgundy, France, taking up a tenth of an acre just inside the base of the deer fence.

My vegetable garden is at a higher elevation than the little vineyard, so I can look down through what we have named "the park," a band of tall oak trees, and watch Michael at work while I putter and tend. Yesterday I was harvesting the last of the radicchio, peeling off the tough outer leaves and uncovering tender burgundy and white globes at the center that brighten up a winter salad. I also gathered the jagged sawteeth of Japanese mizuna and the first flowerettes of mache. I thinned the arugula and winter red romaine seedlings, root and all, and pulled tiny weeds before they enveloped the strawberries and new lettuce and spinach seedlings. And I picked a perfect specimen of flat-headed cabbage, its light green core surrounded by a dark green bonnet of leaves like flower

petals opening from bud, and I brought it with a ribbon as a bouquet to our hosts at the New Year's Eve dinner last night.

The composition of the ground is so different here on my new hilltop. It is light, granular and porous, as if it came from eons of time and weather wearing away the solidity of the mountain behind the house. And it is rich from centuries of leaf mold decomposing in the woods and decades of horses grazing on the pastures and leaving their fertilizer behind. It reflects how much lighter I feel inside. The grief and sadness I carried for so many years has dissolved; the heavy dense clay of longing has given way to intense gratitude for my life.

My garden grew lush and abundant last summer with very little intrusion from pests. Mole tunnels and gopher mounds let me know that a thriving population is making itself at home underground, but the moles have yet to topple over plants in their insect foraging, and the gophers have yet to prefer the roots and stems of my vegetables to their diet before my arrival. I no longer cloud my celebration of the present harmony and abundance with anticipatory anxiety for future possible mishaps.

When I weeded the preexisting landscaping last spring, before Michael built the deer fence, I found nubs of ceanothus and gaura, hardy native plants, eaten back by deer before they could ever spread their wings. And I watched the rosebush by the front deck send out succulent new shoots that systematically disappeared in the night just as the new flower buds formed. So before we could begin the dream of bringing the land to life with nourishment and beauty, we needed deer protection.

Michael built upon the existing corral boundary, raising it, adding welded fencing wire, then affixing wire strands at the top. I helped monitor uncoiling the wire strands, because the wire can turn upon itself in a chaotic jumble if it isn't guided to unfold circle by circle. It was metaphoric, that job. Working together in rhythm, communicating through the tension vibrating in the wire, his having to pace his moving ahead in harmony with my releasing each round from the coiled length.

Today, as I sit at my desk at the beginning of this new year, I am feeling inward and reflective. I connect the tasks here with my life on Mount Veeder twenty years ago. They look the same on the outside, yet feel so different internally. The deer fence at Mount Veeder felt like it separated me from the world outside. Now I appreciate how the fence contains my world within it.

As Michael walked the fencing wire away from me to the furthest post, it made an open spiral. I can visualize that spiral as an airy tunnel in my mind's eye, stretching back across two decades, each loop a cycle around the seasons, connecting the strands of our lives and their recurring lessons of inner transformation. Those tender shoots of awareness that germinated in that long-gone garden have come to fruitful harvest here. Their roots penetrate deeper into inner ground of mind and spirit, their leaves spread wide to embrace broad horizons across the globe. And the ground continually contains the same lessons as the original garden ground: be still, be open, be present, witness "what is" without judgment, let go, and trust what grows naturally in the space.

I see from today's perspective that the strand of motherhood reached almost the whole distance, if not in the foreground, then buried deeply; the same length of time it would have taken to raise and launch a healthy living child.

One of the most poignant times it surfaced was January 1976: a phone call from a pediatrician friend offering us a newborn to adopt if we would be at the hospital by seven o'clock the next morning. Excitement. Terror. A sleepless night, each of us in our own separate worlds, meeting the decision. I, despite fear, say yes. Michael cannot. I witness genuine suffering in his eyes when he tells me he had wanted so to meet me in my desire, but he was unable. His vulnerability, his pain, touches my heart so deeply that in a moment of heart-wrenching compassion I let go of even going to see the child. Letting go, over and over.

For the next few years the prominent strands were our business partnership and my finding an outlet for creative energies apart from nurturing a child or "fitting in as needed," as the tour book to wineries of the Napa Valley described my role at Mount Veeder. Our wines by now had been released successfully to an enthusiastic and appreciative public.

I found a night-school silk-screening class. While most of the participants decorated T-shirts, I used one of my vineyard photographs, which was transformed by the screening process into a dramatic print that everyone loved. The poster I had reproduced from it took on a life of its own, earning me enough money to answer the restlessness within to wander independently without having to justify it in the household budget or to my rational mind.

In 1978 I fulfilled my longing to travel to Nepal and India, no longer as escape, but rather as celebration. I wandered freely for four months, as if in a waking dream, experiencing the effects of my inner reactivity or receptivity on my perception of the outer world with the heightened clarity that traveling outside familiar territory brings. All the significant strands of my life were touched and deepened.

I sought out S. N. Goenka, my friend's meditation teacher, and strengthened the strand of mindful attention, which had opened in the garden, on the South Asian soil where the seeds had originated. Ten days of sitting with myself in the fashion of my short time in Big Sur made it very clear that there is looking and there is "looking!" at what is happening inside. Just sitting watching breath and the passing phenomena of mind and body made it indelibly clear that nothing lasts, everything is constantly changing; suffering is in direct relation to how much we resist the truth of the moment. "Is law of nature," said Goenka.

I witnessed the humblest task being turned into a creative act of devotion by a snack seller on a railway platform at three in the morning. I witnessed how fear is a thought, only present before or after the fact, as I scaled a flimsy bamboo ladder down a precipice or crossed a swinging bridge over a raging river like the one that had appeared in my nightmares. I saw grapevines trying to grow at nine thousand feet in the Himalayas. I was touched by simple loving families who embraced me with their harmony. I identified with the story of the grieving mother who took her dead son to the Buddha and asked him to bring the child back to life. "Bring me mustard seed from houses who have known no death," the Buddha instructed, "and I will grant your desire." In her search, the mother came to realize no such house existed, and in that awareness came her acceptance.

The cultures overthrew any ideas I may have had about what constitutes riches. I saw how simple basic human needs are. I saw the transformational power of bringing one's whole being to whatever one's circumstances were and how love and creativity and harmony emerged so naturally from that acceptance.

I would never walk with the regal posture of the village women I saw balancing water jugs on their heads, no matter how many times my mother had pushed back my shoulders and told me to stand up straight. But unlike the Nepali vintner who was so proud of his oxidized grape wine and so dismissive of the delicious apricot brandy that he made from the wild apricots growing on the way to the vineyard, I could recognize that my task was to put my

heart into my equivalent of his apricot brandy, not into
what could not thrive under my growing conditions.

I returned ready to trust and celebrate my life with Michael
as it was, even without children, with the winery and the
vineyard as its structure. But my absence of four months
had forced Michael to begin sorting things out, and he went
off on a month's vacation shortly after I returned, leaving
me with the responsibilities of the ranch and the winery. I
gained appreciation of the daily pressures he had been feeling. He became aware for himself that our lives had been
out of balance, that the vineyard and winery were his protective fortress against grief and that the fortress had
turned into a prison. He wanted to free himself from the
business.

And so layers began to open out and life changed shape,
though the strands and substance stayed the same. It was
like the onion a Bombay vendor had given me as a spontaneous gift, an onion visually transformed into a lotus
blossom, with its layered petals opening to the core, yet an
onion nonetheless.

I enrolled in graduate school to study psychology and gain broader understanding of my experiences with travel, grief and growth. Michael took up flying, which I saw as his equivalent of meditation. I returned to my garden notes from 1975. Michael spearheaded a move off the property in an attempt to have more distance from the overwhelming day to day responsibilities of the winery. I was surprised at the ease with which I was able to move on once I honored the house and the land with a ceremonial good-bye. In a dream of that time: "I was in my study editing the garden journal when my mother quietly set a brown paper bag outside the door. In it were fireplace ashes. Wonderful! I thought. I will spread them on the garden and they will make good fertilizer for whatever grows next."

Just as we began redirecting our lives toward more balance, we were offered the remaining Mount Veeder parcel of land that Mr. Moyer's widow had been living on, and we had to buy it to integrate the property and its resources. It was clear to both of us that the acquisition was necessary but counter to the direction our lives were taking, so we decided to offer the entire venture, winery and land, for sale.

By 1984 a new owner had established himself and we had fulfilled our consulting commitment to him to share all we knew. I had obtained my master's degree in psychology and was ready to begin an internship to become a marriage and family counselor. Michael wanted to just take off for a few years and travel the wide world. I wanted to pursue my new career. To honor both our needs, we agreed to travel half the year, and I found work situations that allowed me to come and go.

For the next several years we circled the globe and I took steps to gain a license to practice psychotherapy, opened a private practice and felt the biological clock ticking. Michael took on the role of househusband, considered himself unemployed rather than retired, planned more trips and avoided mention of Jason or the possibility of another child. I made one last attempt to resolve the issue. Michael made it very clear that the subject was closed for him, but he lovingly set me free, if that was what I truly needed to fulfill myself, to seek resolution elsewhere.

I was back at the crossroads, "Do you want a baby or to leave him?"—the question that began the journey. This time the question became "Do you want a baby or to stay with him?" I could not have both. I was back to the dilemma faced in the prophetic dream of being bitten by the snake, having to choose a course of healing for myself between two possibilities, each fraught with risk, with Michael unable to help me. Snakes shed the past by shedding their skins.

I entered therapy to help me meet my decision with consciousness and clarity. We began with the issue of children, which then led back to partnership and ultimately to the core of my heart and soul. I met grief, anger, fear and thwarted creativity at deeper and deeper levels every step of the way. A dream from that time conveyed the quality of our marital relationship: Michael and I live in two houses next door to each other. His is neat and orderly. Mine is a jumble. Central to mine is an altar to Jason.
We open windows from time to time and chat with each other. And we invite each other to visit from time to time. He is not comfortable amidst my disorder or in the presence of the altar. I find the order in his house sterile. I realize that I want my house in order, but my kind of order, not his.

A year later, on a vacation with Michael, on a street corner in Assisi, Italy, the dam of sorrow broke and out spilled all the tears of sadness, no longer just for myself, but for all suffering, all loss and separation, for grief itself.

The trigger was witnessing three young mothers stopping their baby carriages to say hello to each other and to admire each other's *bambini*. Tears just wouldn't stop. Tears from my womb, from the very source of fulfillment of my gender. Italy reveres children. These young women took motherhood for granted; to me they had created miracles. I felt my failure to fulfill my traditional creativity as a woman. I asked Michael if he had harbored any sense of blaming me for my not having been able to bear a healthy child. If anything, he shared, he blamed himself. More tears for the burden we had each carried in isolation. Michael shared his concern that I would take my pain to the grave. This time I did not hear critical judgment, as I had felt in past confrontations. This time I trusted that he had come to accept me as I am. "I have never stood in the way of your fulfilling your mothering in other ways, have I?" he asked with genuine concern. I had to look inside myself for the answer. How much effort had I really put out to gather children in my life in other capacities, apart from enjoying my niece and nephew and our friends' children? The truth: not much. The child who had needed nurturing was the child within myself.

And even in relationship to Jason, I had been silent. In focusing on my sense of loss, I had ceased to honor that relationship. I needed to reconnect. I reclaimed being his mother. He would have been twenty years old.

I began to write letters. Here is the one I wrote on his twenty-first birthday:

March 13, 1991

Dear Jason,

It is your twenty-first birthday. How are we to celebrate? Our friends all take out a vintage bottle of the year of their child's birth. We have one bottle of '70 Chateau Bernstein left. It's stored in the wine locker, which Dad can't get into today, though he winced at the thought of drinking it under any circumstances. Something about keeping the last bottle.

Twenty-one years. Maturity. In my life, you are inextricably bound to the garden. I wanted to plant today, and maybe I still will, but the earth is soaked from a much-needed rain last night. The sun is out now, and the wind is icy from the north. I picked a flower bouquet of what little is in bloom—a daffodil, a few violas, the first open ranunculus—to put on the makeshift altar in front of your picture, the only one I have in color of you in your blue fuzzy playsuit on a sunny winter day, delighting with a gleeful smile over a ripe lemon as if you had your own personal sun. I wanted a ceremony, and I just let it evolve spontaneously. As I was lighting a candle in front of the flowers and your photo, I sensed your Dad, curious and respectful, standing behind me in the hall, and I invited him in. He silently made a loving gesture and gave me a gentle kiss and left. This is not his world, but he touches me deeply for joining me in a way he is comfortable, yet leaving me alone.

When I made my request for a 1970 wine for tonight, Dad voiced the resistance I had expected, but then hearing the meaning it would have for me symbolically, he began calling around to locate a bottle of '70 vintage. I heard him say to a friend, "It would have been our son's twenty-first birthday had he lived." Tears welled up. It is your birthday, whether you can celebrate with us or not. The tears were good tears, for hearing the words from him, his joining me in acknowledgment.

Letting you back into his life, our life together. When I thanked him tenderly after he was off the phone, he let our eyes meet for a moment, and in his too were the emotion and the love that joined us originally to conceive you. I felt our sacred connection.

I joined your spirit in the garden. Dad came out to check on me a few times before he went off to fetch the wine. I was fashioning a little ritual space where I could gather a representative of each season and each stage of growth—seeds and sprouts, buds and flowers, blooming and fading dissolving back to compost—and the diverse forms growth takes— weeds and flowers, vegetables and tree leaves, feeling the force of life that leaps across time and space. I scattered red poppy seeds and winter romaine lettuce and flowering broccoli until the clouds turned mauve and gray with just a tinge of pink from the setting sun.

At dinner we made a toast to you and to us. A part of my heart stayed closed to your father when he could not let you be part of our lives. Tonight I felt as if we were a family again. The two of us, and your spirit.

I cherish you, Jason, wherever you are.

On the twentieth anniversary of his death, April 21, I returned to Mount Veeder, again feeling the pull to mark the day ceremonially. I came to tend the flowering cherry tree I had planted twenty years earlier in Jason's memory. It had struggled over the years, been bruised and wounded in brushes with a tractor, starved for water and nourishment once we no longer lived on the property. In spite of its stress, it had managed to send out a few blossoms, which had just opened. At the earth line a strong healthy rootstock shoot had emerged. The new growth symbolized for me new energy coming from the same source as my mothering but not necessarily tied to my child—nurturing and creativity renewing in the present. I wandered the property, gathering a bouquet to place as an offering at the base of the tree: purple myrtle flowers from around the winery where I first encountered the dream snake who had come to symbolize my spiritual awakening; calendulas and rosebuds, which were all that remained of my garden. I lit incense and filled a little pouch with dried rosemary and hung it in the tree to signify leaving behind the sorrow that I have carried. I placed a large granite rock before the flowers, with pebbles and sand on it to symbolize the gradual dissolving of even the most impenetrable grief. Then I scattered seeds of my beloved red poppies around the entire base of the tree. I could feel my heart opening, swelling with love, finally understanding that letting go of the sense of loss and deprivation did not diminish the place in my heart belonging to my child. When I returned home, I began turning the soil in my backyard, laying out a border of marigold seeds, imagining them the structure in which a new garden would flourish.

A few months later, on vacation, gliding in a *makoro* (canoe) in the Okavango Delta in Botswana searching for *tsitatunga,* the illusive deer-like creature whose splashes we heard in the distance as he "walked on water," I found myself drawn to the depths of the clear water, tracing the roots of the water lilies down to the sandy bottom where they were anchored. Gliding in the utter stillness, overcome suddenly by emotion, I felt an aching tenderness as my heart wrenched open, and I heard it say, "I forgive me." Through the tears I felt a sense of release, of acceptance, for all the years it had taken to come to peace.

On the twenty-first anniversary of Jason's death, I wrote him again:

April 21, 1992

Dear Jason,

The flowers I brought to you today, or to our connection place at the ranch, your tree, are all from my garden. I didn't think of past, present, future, seasons, stages. I just responded to the now, the incredible beauty and variety right in my yard. Huge orange-red oriental poppies with black centers, ranunculus in full flower, roses in first bloom, columbine sending starbursts out and making seedpods all at the same time. Purple statice and pink azalea, red and yellow geum, rockrose and Dutch iris; even a shirley poppy, and of course calendula. I added some tree shoots and some shrub shoots and a sprig of oregano.

Mount Veeder was deserted, but nobody has changed the lock combination, so I had no trouble letting myself in. The ranch has a new owner again, and last time we had gone up, Flossie, Dad's giant schnauzer I gave him years ago, had still been there. We hadn't had the heart to confine her to a suburban backyard when we'd moved. She had given her watchdog growl for a moment, then had stopped, seemed to recognize Dad, and whimpered, rubbed up against his leg, and jumped for joy, bringing tears to both of us. She's gone now, buried under the redwoods. Everything was so quiet there, only the birds and the rush of wind. As I drove up to the house and got out of the car, my heart dropped. Your tree has died and been cut down. The new shoot from the side is still there, but it is coming from below the graft line, so it has no flowers. The rosebuds I brought have already begun to open and the geum to droop, so the burst of lively color may only be for a moment. I offer the abundance of the moment. That's all any of us can do, isn't it? Life is a continual embracing and letting go. Good bye, child.

On our thirtieth wedding anniversary that August, along with the Zoo Doo ("gourmet" garden fertilizer from elephant and rhino at the Memphis Zoo), I received a handwritten note from Michael expressing his deep love and appreciation, acknowledging the wide range of our shared years together: "From deep love to despair, from extreme happiness to depression, from understanding to insensitivity, and from mutual sharing to independent activities, our relationship has endured and even prospered in the face of tragedies that tear so many relationships apart." The prison walls of protection had melted. "I love so many of your qualities, but it is your smile that brings tears when I think of you in your absence. I love and cherish you very deeply and consider myself the luckiest person alive to have been in your life for thirty years. I would like to stay a little longer." And so he has, welcomed now and embraced and appreciated.

When I introduce myself and tell my story at the women's retreats my friend Ellie and I have been facilitating for the past five years, I usually say I have had several marriages, all of them with Michael. This one is the fruition of the others, the genuine partnership of equals, with mutual appreciation, each contributing what we have to give for the benefit of the whole. And together we are cultivating our new garden.

Many years ago I had a dream that I lived in a barracks. A little boy who lived across the street invited me into his mansion. As he took me through the ground floor, I understood this is where daily life was lived. On the second floor I heard a voice: This is for spiritual life, but emphatically, "No church!" On the top floor, the voice: This is for joy and celebration, but "No theatre!" I wanted to live in that house.

My dream has come true. I have come to live in that expansive place, inside and out. My new hilltop feels like paradise. The emphatic voice reminds me not to cling to or try to structure the form of spirit, joy and celebration, but to meet them in their aliveness, which means their ever-changing fluidity.

As the strands of wire on the fence are pulled, each to its full length, the spiral shrinks until finally it disappears into a straight line. With the wire tautly fixed to the fence post, the circle is complete. On the fence, the strands are separate and distinguishable. In my life, they have intermingled to weave a whole.

Rain, rain, rain; day after day of rain; three weeks now of rain. Whipping wind rushing through the trees, sending raindrops blowing by my study window in horizon-

tal sheets, then cloudbursts relentlessly beating down vertically on the asphalt with such force the drops bounce up like dancing jellybeans. The whoosh of water pours out of the sky; constant drips pour out of the downspouts. Then slow, steady, beating drops, hour after hour. The banks of the Napa River and tributary creeks have overflowed. Napa Valley is on the national television news. I went to my office to see clients on Tuesday and found sandbags piled against all the ground-level entrances. The door to my office is up a small flight of stairs, so it was unobstructed. The parking lot had a layer of mud. When a client on Mount Veeder canceled because the road was blocked with mudslides, I wondered if it was our old terraces on the road, as they had been in 1986.

At home here I am safe. The ground has absorbed all the moisture. The warm days, when the storms came up from the El Niño current in the Pacific, coaxed all measure of mushroom forms from the land. Yellow, brown, grayish white. Enormous umbrellas, caps, hoods popping out of the pasture and oak stumps, a sea of tiny inky caps spreading across the topsoil of my garden extension.

Today the mist is hanging in the steep hills behind our house in ribbons of subtly different shades of gray, like the calligraphic washes of an Oriental scroll painting. Barely a breeze is stirring in this gray, utterly still suspension of time. The temperature has dropped. The next front is expected from the Arctic. Michael's become stir-crazy, unable to get outside to plant the fruit trees that were delivered, so he went off to the movies. I stayed home to write.

It's past lunchtime, my stomach tells me. Michael, the family chef since I began working, has left the makings of salad he always prepares for lunch. But the bone-chilling dampness says "soup" to me. I remember having put a container of leftover chicken broth in the refrigerator from last night's dinner, and I know I have a row of cilantro in the garden, maybe enough to make *sopa alentejo,* the simple soup I loved from our visit to Portugal, just cilantro and garlic and broth, with an egg poached in it, poured over stale bread in the bottom of each bowl. I bundle up in my parka and take the garden basket I bought from a tribal woman in a remote southwest China market, and when I look over the garden, even though everything I planted in the fall is still small, I can see all kinds of possibilities to add to the cilantro. Thinnings of broccoli rabe, the ancient Roman vegetable with slightly bitter broccoli flavor that is more leaves and stems than flower buds; the two kinds of kale, whose outer leaves are large enough to harvest, made more tender by the frosts they've encountered between deluges of rain; parsley; mustard green thinnings; a small cabbage head; and a fennel bulb with fluffy frond peeking from the center. My fingers are freezing, so I snap off leaves quickly or poke my fingers in the gritty sandy soil to grasp thinnings by the roots. I could wear gloves, but I love the feel of the earth, the grit, between my fingers without an intermediary. It amazes me that after so much rain, the soil still shakes off the roots easily and I can walk between the planted rows without any mud sticking to my garden boots.

I feel a quickening of excitement and anticipation as I gather the abundance so I can run back to the warm house and blow my runny nose and warm my fingertips. My imagination is combining the ingredients. I have garlic we harvested in the summer and minced in the food processor and then froze in individual ice tray cubes; it can join the shallot and olive oil I'll sauté the chopped greens in. While chopping the cabbage, I think back to another Portuguese soup, *caldo verde*, and that gives me the idea to microwave a potato and use it as thickening. And that takes me back to the Portuguese farm family who served us the soup in their cozy kitchen in the middle of a vineyard and to the woman of that house, who gave me the seeds of the special cabbage that grows to people-sized stalks. My heart is dancing with the feeling of connectedness across time and space, with the fullness and appreciation of generosity of spirit those people shared, and with anticipation for the nourishment simmering on the stove top. I sample the greens simmering in the broth. They are tender. I toss in the chopped cilantro and immediately incorporate the mashed potato, first stirring some broth into the potato, then adding the smooth mixture to the pot. I have my cheerful placemat set with my favorite bowl and spoon, and I feel so full of life and happiness as I serve myself all this goodness that I spontaneously find myself grinning from ear to ear. As I savor the warmth and nourishment of the melding flavors of the greens, with only the cilantro keeping a separate identity, I can hardly contain my joy. I taste the earthiness; I feel the connection with the earth through my cells; I am the earth as I ingest its bountiful goodness.

As I'm washing the bowl after the meal, feeling full and satisfied, I am struck with amazement that I hadn't made the connection earlier. Here I am, for all outward appearances, reliving the rainy winter day twenty years ago when my journey began, but nothing is the same inside! Twenty years ago I saw rain as dreary, reflective of tears and sadness. My earth was heavy and soaked. This year I have witnessed the nuances of rain from day to day and the vast range of its nature, from the gentleness of enshrouding mist to the assertion of relentless downpour, and I have welcomed the receptivity of my soil to the life-giving moisture. My heart is full to overflowing with a smile that lights up all my cells with a dancing tingle. A fountain of gratitude that borders on sacred washes over me. I am bursting with joy. I once had a lucid dream in which I breathed a deep breath that kept entering and entering, and I kept expanding and expanding until I just dissolved into breath. I find myself now having brought both hands to my heart without thinking, as if to check whether I am still here.

When I turn off the kitchen water tap, I still hear a faint background sound of rushing water. The creek! We were told when we purchased the property that the gully would become a creek in the heavy rains. We left that part of the property outside the deer fence for practical reasons. Running water could wash out underneath the fence and then the deer could crawl under the base.

The sound pulls me like a magnet, out the family room door, up the hill by the redwood tree, past the chicken coop I've turned into a potting shed and down a bank into the wild part of the property—woods and tangle and dormant poison oak, with only the oak-leaf-strewn path to the water tank. The sound expands here, and just outside the gate I am in its presence. The water is spilling through the rocks at the property line from the higher elevation above them. It crashes between majestic boulders covered with new bright green moss and collects in clear, relatively still pools at each level where the rocks widen. Then it drops again, with a gentler sound where the distance is not so great and the path narrows. I see new fern fronds beginning to unfold from amidst the moss. All around me are tall oaks skirted in the same brilliant new green moss that embraces the rocks.

I feel sacred presence here, the same feeling of hallowed ground that I had in the Druid groves of the British Isles. I sense the boulders holding the energy and vibration of all time. Raindrops begin to fall. As I stand stone still beside the water, I am outside of time. Tingling inside, I witness water as stream and, at the same time, each raindrop entering the movement, separate, yet indistinguishable from the stream itself. I witness the water as a steady stream and simultaneously as an ever-changing flow cascading down the incline, out to the river, and on to San Francisco Bay.

I stand before the water as a stream, a conduit through which the richness of my life experiences have flowed like the raindrops moving to the sea. My journey these past twenty years has been to become whole, a blossoming, alive and authentic self, a loving, accepting, trusting self. I reverently offer my life's details to the stream, sending them off into the natural flow, feeling light and free. In Nepal, I watched recipients of a Tibetan Buddhist lama's direct mind transmission of enlightenment throw rice into the air immediately after, symbolizing nonattachment, even to the ultimate goal. If you have received enlightenment through this transmission, the rice symbolized "let it go." At this moment I understand the gesture.

I feel the changes in my female body stirring as the reproductive cycle wanes. I am free now to be grandmother, belonging to the whole, because I have no particular grandchild to tend. I am free now to just be. Free to wear my wrinkles and my sags with acceptance. Free to speak, knowing that I no longer need any particular response, trusting the source, which often comes from beyond my knowing. Free to have no purpose beyond being a spark of life living itself with as much awareness as possible, including the awareness of limited awareness. Being kind to myself and others, feeling deep compassion for the suffering others bring me in my work, for I know that the spaciousness I now feel within is the ground beneath their suffering, too, as it was beneath mine—ground just waiting to be cleared. Witnessing the paradox that being unconditionally present with ourselves just as we are, without judgment, holds the key to clearing the ground. Knowing that the denial or distraction with which we fight our suffering, thinking they will outwit the pain and help us survive, are actually creating a whole secondary level of pain, including inner emptiness and self-loathing. We want it not to hurt, but to have hurt fall away, we must embrace it without a trace of resistance. Nature takes its course. Our lives are the process once we get out of our own way.

We grow at the rate we grow. Some of us are morning glories, some giant pines. Each step of the way has its beauty and meaning; there is no rushing the process of coming to full flower. As my asparagus taught me twenty years ago, the only place we'll find the seeds that grow for us are inside ourselves. To be with ourselves in that discovery process is to be still and open, curious and attentive, receptive, without expectation, without preconception, without judging what we find in our hearts, minds, bodies and spirits. When we're constantly reacting, protecting, it is not possible to notice or to choose appropriate action.

In our culture, we have lost meaningful rites of passage that give us a sense of who we are. To come home to ourselves and to life, to realize the illusion of our separateness, to transcend self, we must have a self to transcend. And in the search for self, we discover worlds upon worlds within ourselves reflected back to us in the figure eight of our relationships with others and the external world. We are each the world. And so in the process of coming to peace within, we are contributing to world peace.

Inner peace creates a radiance that is able to beam warmth and well-being to others who come into its presence. I have been in its presence at the hearth of a Nepali family and in a chance meeting with Mother Teresa, when we held hands and giggled like schoolgirls about to dance from the gladness that bounced us up and down. I have felt it in the topography of a Tibetan grandmother's face, leathery crevices of wrinkles so deep that her undoubtedly sparkling eyes were just slits, and in the heart of a volunteer grandmother in the pediatric intensive care ward, beaming calm and caring to us all with her smile.

The kind of smile that comes from an open heart, from joy and gratitude for this life, for all that grows and flourishes, bears its fruit and dies to replenish the ground for new growth. A smile that comes from gratitude for the knowing that we are life as all around us is life. The smile is for life itself, a smile like a sunbeam, unable to be summoned through will. It belongs to life, not to any particular place or person upon whom it shines, or even for that matter to the person through whom it shines.

In moments when a smile like that wells up in my heart and spills over, it is the gift of coming to harvest. And then, when I am spilling over from the fullness, spreading it around is no sacrifice. Sharing the abundance becomes the most natural, spontaneous act.

I awakened this morning with two words echoing: simple, sacred. They say it all.

Life is simple. Breath, inspiration. Expiration, letting go. Eating when you are hungry, sleeping when you are tired. The task before us is to get out of our own way so we are present to meet the truth of the moment. Michael and I delivered some wine in southern California years ago and attended a talk Krishnamurti gave in an oak grove in Ojai. I don't remember what he said, but my impression of walking behind him afterward has stayed with me. There was a palpable stillness, a spaciousness, around him as he stopped to take in the perfume of a flower or to pet a dog, each gesture having the gentle grace of a benediction.

Life is sacred. The traditional people knew it. They had stories. The Mayans (according to the calendar I had in my office last year) saw the earth, the "face of the world," in their language, as the face of the life-sustaining deity; people are flowers that grow from the sacred land, earrings adorning its beautiful face. I love that image.

The sun is shining today for the first time in almost a month, and I'm bursting with energy to get outside. I know just where I want to plant the forsythia, which is a fountain of gold first thing in the spring: right outside my study window. And I need to get a feel for where the bare-root roses will be happiest. I already have tomato and eggplant and pepper seeds potted in a little windowsill greenhouse. I know the sunshine will coax them closer to sprouting, though I don't know when. And I can't wait to get into the garden and turn over the ground to get it ready for the new growing season.

December 2003

Paradises can only be made with our own hands, with our own creativity in harmony with the free creative spirit of nature.

— Hundertwasser

Our land has become a Garden of
Eden, a canvas that nature, Michael,
and I paint upon in plants. Everyone
who visits says, "If I lived here, I'd
never want to leave."

My pomegranate tree grows lush and delicate by the pool-
side arbor, giving shade from the setting summer sun. It
was a gift to me from the man who sold Michael olive
trees. The pomegranate may have been the original tree in
the Garden of Eden, *pomum granatum,* the apple of many
seeds. The pomegranate and the olive, the fig and the vine
all conjure images of the Old Testament Promised Land,
creating heaven on earth. Terra cotta tiles with pomegranate images adorn the pillars holding up the arbor. I made
the tiles, first shaping the squares with a rolling pin, then
rolling out thin coils between my palms and snaking them
upon the flat surface in the shape of the fruit, adding tiny
balls in the heart to represent the seeds. Working with clay,
a dense rich earth, is an extension for me of working garden soil.

The serpent is here too, sunning himself on the top of a

ceramic irrigation box. I love the surprise and fear when people notice him. He's glazed with clear grey green celadon and deep brown mashika. Real snakes abound as well. I find them sleeping under the Mexican sage, cardoon and caper bushes. The snake as symbol has always drawn me to my inner depths just as the complex sweet sour taste of pomegranate bound Persephone in Greek myth to the depths of the underworld.

Pomegranate trees thrive under conditions where other trees would be unable to survive. Hence, they have come to symbolize strength and endurance. In ancient Egyptian and Christian symbology, they represent death and rebirth. In Islamic tradition every pomegranate contains one seed that comes directly from heaven. With all their seeds, they are the ultimate feminine symbol of fertility, fertility that can come in so many forms besides bearing children. Just today I noticed the last globe of the season, cracked open by the alternating warmth and frost of this early December, still hanging on a lower branch of the tree which is now losing its yellowed leaves in the process of going dormant. I open it and gently peel away the protective membrane to savor the delicious juice around the seeds. This act mirrors what I have experienced internally over the years, a gentle peeling away of protective layers to reach the ripened fruit of fulfillment.

One of the first projects here was a stone retaining wall that doubled the size of my vegetable garden. It declared a separation of our two territories, Michael's orderly orchard and vineyard below, my exuberant chaos of vegetables and flowers above. Over the years those boundaries have softened.

In his territory I have gopher-proof, raised beds of arti-chokes and garlic down at the corner of the olive orchard. (Yes, the gophers have discovered the abundance, and if I don't plant in raised beds with welded wire bottoms, I have to plant half-again the quantity we want, for them). I've also built islands of rock meandering among the trees from which caper plants thrive. And in the background I have a row of raspberries supported by wires strung between two oaks. In the midst of the olive orchard I have contributed some very special trees, spirited from Italy— *Olivi dolci*. Sweet olives. No bitterness that needs to be leached in curing.

Michael's wine cellar is in my territory, in the center of the Garden House, a remodeled wreck of an outbuilding that opens onto my vegetable garden. Another part of the building is my studio/potting shed, off limits to his sense of order. "It will save our marriage," I used to tease him. It has in fact alleviated a whole world of tension between us that used to erupt in the kitchen, fueled by things like dirt in the sink from my washing salad greens or on the drainboard when I brought in vegetables directly from the garden. Since it was completed I haven't found any artichokes or eggplants on my office desk or rocking chair, his previous form of non-verbal communication. Now he visits the garden regularly and consults on the mandatory vegetables I want him to use in his cooking.

If this place is a Garden of Eden, does that make us Adam and Eve? Maybe the story somewhat in reverse, for we've lived those biblical edicts of expulsion before we arrived here: the sorrow in bringing forth children, the tilling ground from whence we were fashioned, thy husband ruling over thee, and so forth. We still haven't quite mastered the eternal dance of male and female with all its tension and hilarity, exasperation and moments of sweetness. We danced at a friend's wedding a few years ago. Even the music didn't help much to synchronize our very different rhythms, but at least we tried. In our clumsiness and failure to either lead or follow, we laughed together, undaunted and unselfconscious about our awkwardness.

At our 40th anniversary celebration last year, we had a snapshot blown up to display for our friends. We are each holding up something we are very proud of. Michael is showing off a framed Art Nouveau poster by Alphonse Mucha from around 1900 advertising *Lefevre-Utile Gaufrettes Vanille,* with an enchantress seducing the viewer to buy cookies. I am beaming ear-to-ear, holding a string from which my first successfully trapped gopher dangles. It is still the only gopher I've caught.

Michael has continued to purchase many more posters in Paris. Paris has in fact become a spiritual home for him, as this property is for me. He's written a very well received Paris Guide which requires us to return often for updating. I have had to find a way to keep true to my own rhythm when I'm there, with quiet reflective time and visits with girlfriends to balance joining him in search of the new gardens and art museums, undiscovered bistros and restaurants he writes about.

Ellie and I still gather groups of women together for the kind of soul nourishment and self-discovery that only women seem to do together. We search out the common threads in our lives and ask the questions that lead to finding our own clear and authentic voices. The same themes seem to compel us all, whether we have children or not, whether we have husbands or not. What has stood in the way of our realizing our beauty, our creativity, our power, our gifts to share? What keeps us, as Voltaire so aptly put it centuries ago, from "cultivating our gardens"?

I've returned to that same yellow pad I sat down with in 1975 and I found a dialogue that I hadn't previously included in *Growing Season.* "Why am I writing all this?" I had asked. The answer: "I'm writing this for all of us who are not going to be great poets or artists or carefree women of the world. We have to get over our inferiority complexes and self protections so we can realize that the quality of attention we pay to our activities and the enjoyment we derive from them are what give them meaning, not how others judge their worth." Then, in bold capital letters I proclaimed across the page—

MAKE YOUR LIFE YOUR WORK OF ART!

That's what I've been doing these past nine years.

The gift Jason gave us was to see the fragility of life, the NOWness of it. With each year I have the same lessons, those deep truths unearthed from my garden ground, renewed and reaffirmed. Homemade compost, nature's breaking down the past, keeps fertilizing and enriching the garden soil, just as a similar process takes place within to continue opening my heart.

Just this morning, as I walked my dog Posey by the neighboring horse ranch, I noticed a huge compost pile, and Miguel offered me a load of aged horse manure, which he home delivered this afternoon. Abundance beyond my wildest dreams!

Acknowlegments

Just as the garden taught that things grow in their own   179
time, so this book slowly evolved thanks to the love,
encouragement and skills of so many friends and col-
leagues. Eleanor Coppola, Pam Hunter, Margit Jacob, Niki
Singer and Michael Sheets, Lucy Simon Levine, Michelle
Turner, Carol Field, Sue Bender, Mirka Knaster, Suzanne
Simpson, Anita Feder-Chernila, Bonnie Strauss, Sharon
Smith, Carolyn Miller, Julie Bennett, Tamara Traeder and
Roy Carlisle, among them.

As it first sent its ripples out into the world, it brought feed-
back to complete the communication circle every author
dreams of, the farthest being from Horiko Horiguchi who
read the book in Japanese translation with true understanding, affirming for me that its essence transcends barri-
ers of language and geography. Among other new and old
friends, Lilla Weinberger, Margaret Kaufman, Bunnie
Finkelstein, Charleen Steen, Don Kay and Bonnie Levinson,
Margaret Gokey, Jane Meyers, Violetta Sternberg , Suzie
Rashkis, Carol Adrienne, Tom Nemcik, Priscilla Ulene and

my dear sister, Barbara Trachtenberg, have provided enthusiastic support and shining lights.

And now, thanks to Paulette Millichap, Ja-lene Clark and Sally Dennison at Council Oak, this new edition, like a perennial, returns to life. Tamara Traeder and Diana Morley have made it enjoyable to create the Afterword. Patricia Curtan serendipitously visited the garden, spotted my hand-painted tiles waiting in the potting shed to be put in place on the pillars outside and said, "There's your cover image!" Nancy Shapiro's skilled layout and design translated it to the new cover.

Then, of course, there's dear Michael, by my side even when we've been looking in different directions. His desire to return to the land began this new growing season, and he's become as much my subject matter as the garden.

Thank you all!

Notes

1. Ranier Marie Rilke, quoted by Ann Morrow Lindbergh in *Gift from the Sea* (New York: Random House, Vintage Books, 1978), p. 97–8.

2. Ibid., p. 94.

3. Jiddu Krishnamurti, *Freedom from the Known* (New York: Harper and Row, 1969), p. 83–4.

4. Jiddu Krishnamurti, *Education and the Significance of Life* (New Delhi, India: B.I. Publications, 1973), p. 128.

About the Author

Arlene Bernstein is a licensed psychotherapist who has taught meditation and facilitated workshops and women's retreats based on the principles discovered in her garden.

She and her husband Michael established Mount Veeder Winery in the hills above Napa Valley, California in the early 1970s. Since the sale of the winery, Arlene has divided her time between her private practice and her garden, when she is not traveling the world with Michael. Ms. Bernstein is a cum laude graduate of UCLA, has an M.A. in Art with a focus on Photography from San Francisco State University and an M.A. in Psychology from Sonoma State University.